DECODING BUSINESS MINDS

Praise for the Book

Our young aspirants in business and entrepreneurship need to develop an innovative spirit. I'm deeply appreciative of Ajay Gupta's endeavour to play the role of catalyst and inspire businessmen.

—Vijay Rupani, former Chief Minister, Gujarat

Ajay Gupta's zeal to make India 'Atmanirbhar' is infectious and he takes pride in sharing this mission with others. His book offers invaluable learnings for entrepreneurs who want to chase their dreams and achieve success.

—Sandeep Aggarwal, author and Founder of ShopClues and Droom

It is a must-read for students, budding entrepreneurs and start-up founders alike.

—Nipun Aggarwal, Senior Vice President, Tata Sons

Drawn from real-life experiences, Ajay Gupta's writing is honest and refreshing and this is a perfect guide for anyone who wants to start a business in India.

—N.K. Chaudhary, Chairman and Managing Director, Jaipur Rugs

The beautiful dream offered by this book to millions will surely not allow them to sleep. An incredible book!

—N.D. Gupta, Member of Parliament, Rajya Sabha

Decoding Business Minds is truly a businessman's book in every sense. It has something to offer every Indian.

—Manish Aggarwal, Director, Bikanervala Foods Pvt. Ltd

India is at the cusp of change and a lot of economic growth is happening. This book will help people who want to do business to contribute to the economy and create a positive impact in the society.

—V.K. Arora, Managing Director, LT Foods, Daawat Basmati Rice

Decoding Business Minds is significantly powerful and motivating.

—Himanshu Gupta, CEO and Director, Moneywise Financial Services Pvt. Ltd

The book develops you and takes you to the level where it unlocks the potential of becoming an influential businessman. I am sure that it will assist the people of India to look at business not as an option but as a career.

—Dr Kanubhai Tailor, President, Disable Welfare Trust of India, Padma Shri awardee

In this book, Ajay Gupta has magnificently captured his refined business acumen of three decades to illuminate and awaken the entrepreneur in us. It serves an offering to everyone who is or might one day venture into his or her own business.

—Jeev Milkha Singh, renowned golfer, and Padma Shri and Arjuna awardee

DECODING BUSINESS MINDS

UNLEASHING THE POWER OF WEALTH CREATION

AJAY GUPTA

RUPA

Published by
Rupa Publications India Pvt. Ltd 2022
7/16, Ansari Road, Daryaganj
New Delhi 110002

Sales Centres:
Allahabad Bengaluru Chennai
Hyderabad Jaipur Kathmandu
Kolkata Mumbai

ISBN: 978-93-91256-65-4

First impression 2022

10 9 8 7 6 5 4 3 2 1

To everyone...
Together we can transform ourselves,
our families, society and the country at large.

CONTENTS

FOREWORD

It is indeed very satisfying to write the foreword for a very fresh and distinctive book which has redefined the role of businessmen in India. For the first time, our countrymen will get an insightful book that connects well to every businessman irrespective of his business segment and size of venture.

Ajay Gupta, the author, is one of the most influential businessmen of India who has future-oriented mindset and works incessantly to achieve his goals. He is already well known nationwide specially for providing quality education through Bachpan playschools, Academic Heights Public Schools and because of his thoughtful step in the higher education segment with Rishihood University.

His book *Decoding Business Minds* is a treasure-trove of valuable business lessons that are the outcome of Ajay's own business experiences in diverse segments.

This powerful book is divided in 36 chapters that strive to decode the business mind. These chapters comprise interesting anecdotes that are used to explain different stages in the life cycle of business in simple and easy-to-understand language. In other words, it is a ready reckoner for small- and mid-size business owners aiming to take their businesses to the next level using ready-to-implement strategies. It will prepare them for a long business journey which is a mix of challenges, opportunities, risk, reward and a lot more.

Read this book at any point of time as it can give wings to your dreams. Every line will help you learn more and more about *business, business* and *business.* It is a must-read not just for aspiring and existing businessmen but for all youngsters as it would inspire them to choose business as a career and grow it innovatively.

This book is a medium as well as a stepping stone to create Atmanirbhar Bharat. It encourages individuals to think beyond jobs and build a country of entrepreneurs who are not only capable of creating a market for themselves but also generate employment for others.

Ajay is marching ahead with a great vision to make India *business wala desh, khushiyon wala desh.* Of course, India needs more and more businesses and businessmen. I wish him all the best.

Suresh Prabhu

Member of Parliament, Rajya Sabha, Government of India, and former Minister of Civil Aviation, Railways, Commerce and Industry, Government of India

PREFACE

India needs aggressive businessmen!

The idea behind writing this book is to share my significant learning experiences and help business aspirants and entrepreneurs across the world, whether they are already established or fledgling. I hope this book will serve as a lighthouse for business persons to sail through the darkest hours of volatility, uncertainty, complexity and ambiguity and emerge as effective and thoughtful leaders.

This is a ready reckoner for business persons at any stage of business, whether they are stuck in taking forward a business idea or confused in their plans for expansion of business.

India has always been a country of businessmen and traders. Even with little to no formal education or training, merchants and traders in premodern India have always known and practised the art and science of doing business. Almost by default, these men and women cultivated business acumen and skills to rival modern-day business schools. Business was, so to say, in their genes.

The arrival of the British in India marked a sea change. The economy transitioned into one rife with inequality. After colonization, the business instinct that was once so inherent in the children of this nation was buried. India became a country of consumers.

Throughout this book, I strive to change this.

I want to awaken these sleeping business instincts within the country's youngsters. I want their dormant genes to come alive, allowing them to polish their acumen and loudly revive 'Make in India'. I strongly believe that India needs thousands upon thousands of new businessmen, charting new paths in every nook and corner of our country to meet the ever-growing needs and expectations of our population. I believe that these needs will be met by young and aspiring men and women. In fact, I believe that women entrepreneurs will take India to the next level in years to come.

In my opinion, Indians are not only capable of building big businesses rapidly like Ola, Swiggy, etc., but also have the ability to nurture and grow small businesses and make them big eventually. It is enough to start a business that has been tried and tested, and which has been succeeding over many decades. I believe that it is of utmost necessity to develop a spirit to do what has been done before, but in a more exciting manner; one must do something that is different, simple, and yet innovative.

Adopting this approach will truly make India *atmanirbhar* in every aspect. We will be self-sufficient and empowered to help in the process of nation-building. My desire is simply that this book plays the role of a catalyst.

This book is based on more than three decades of experience in business. I have taken pains to include some key learnings for aspiring and existing businessmen, presenting them in the form of anecdotes, in the hope that the stories will illuminate and urge individuals to reflect on their business and their inherent business acumen. I have made every effort to ensure that the information covers different aspects of the life cycle of businesses in India (in particular) and in the world (in general). I want the youth of India to realize that it is passion that transforms, that makes ideas into marketable products and services.

I am certain that reading this book will motivate readers to start, sustain and grow their businesses. On my part, I undertake that I shall always be available to help aspiring businessmen, bringing my diverse experience and knowledge to mentor willing individuals to bring about change in many aspects of their businesses.

I wish all my readers and the business fraternity good luck to keep up their hard work and succeed!

1

PREGNANCY AND BUSINESS

Neha went for a prenatal check-up in the last trimester of her pregnancy.

'Any problems?' the doctor asked.

She was ready with her long unending list of complaints.

'Yes,' she began, 'I am not at all comfortable while sitting. I can't eat what I really want to eat. I feel like vomiting most of the time. I am uncomfortable while sleeping horizontally and even when I turn on my side. I have to go to the washroom too often. I have headaches and I'm sore from the baby's kicking and my feet are all swollen ...'

The doctor patiently listened while thoroughly examining her. He nodded, evidently sympathetic towards Neha's difficulties. Finally, he turned around and announced, 'No complaints,' leaving Neha shocked.

After that, the doctor pressed the bell, indicating the nurse to send in the next patient. The doctor knew quite well that all the symptoms that Neha had described were quite normal, in fact, they were desirable for anyone in Neha's position, wanting a healthy child.

Many such *normal* mid-sized businesses in India are in a position like Neha's. As a businessman running a mid-sized business, one has to bear with typical governmental policies, a high percentage of taxes, multiplicity of regulatory controls, complex accounting procedures, confusing tax structures, conventional labour laws, cut-throat competition, lack of favourable business laws, unnecessary government intervention, perhaps even a continuation of the infamous licence raj and its tedious systems of acquiring business loans, lack of clarity about various policies, frequent changes in those policies, etc.

Believe me, the list is very long, but don't lose heart. After all, you are a businessman operating in India, your beloved motherland.

In the story, Neha is in her last trimester. Soon, she will give birth to a baby; one she has nurtured in her womb for nine months. The baby's birth will be an ecstatic moment for Neha; she will be on the top of the world. Can there be any more joyous moment ever in the world for Neha? What greater feeling than bringing a life into this world?

My dear businessman, you too have to learn to be very patient with the birth of your children. The sooner you learn to accept the challenges during conception and your long pregnancy, the better it will be for you and for business.

You and I have a great responsibility on our shoulders and we must bear it with great perseverance and pride. We have to tread this difficult path and make our own way for ourselves. Based on my experience, I can say confidently that it is indeed possible for us to accomplish this glory, now more than ever before.

Long ago, it was believed that every engineering aspirant have spectacles perched on their nose. When I was a small child, both my paternal and my maternal grandmothers said that a schoolgoing boy wearing spectacles would 'essentially' pursue engineering. A boy without spectacles would raise doubts. How could he pursue a career in engineering in such a state?

Certainly, both my grandmothers understood that there was no proven connection whatsoever between the wearing of spectacles and the pursuit of an education in engineering. The spectacles neither gave admission in an engineering college, nor did they guarantee a job. They must have known that there was no logic behind such a saying. So what was the basis for their belief?

My grandmothers had seen most (if not all) engineers with their trademark wide-rimmed spectacles. The wearing of spectacles became a tell-tale mark of being an engineer.

Taking this analogy forward, I would say that there are some tell-tale marks to indicate that you are a businessman. To begin with, like almost every other businessman, you too have a long and hectic working schedule, you too are somewhat disorganized in your approach towards doing things and you always have some pending tasks that need to be attended to—on an urgent basis.

You invariably have a list of 'unanswered' phone calls that you must urgently return, you are perennially looking for additional funds to plough into your venture, you are generally struggling with your income tax and other returns to various government agencies/departments, you are generally required to meet your legal advisors regularly and you are always looking for ways to circumvent the various laws that apply to your business.

Your list of pains and troubles could be still longer.

Despite the odd and rather undesirable tell-tale marks, I would say that if you are a businessman in India, then you are indeed very fortunate. Just look at all the advantages that we have to succeed in India.

The enormous population of our country poses a distinct advantage when it comes to businesses. The number of people travelling via trains running across the country at any given point of time can easily surpass the total population of many countries of the world. Such a population presents an opportunity—a higher consumption rate and a higher demand for products and services.

There are other advantages peculiar to the nature and circumstance of Indians.

In general, Indians are a forgetful and forgiving lot. We give out second chances to many organizations that have once given us inferior quality products and services. Such a mindset allows people to lead a relatively stress-free life and to live in the present moment. This is a highly desirable situation for any uncertain business.

Indians are adaptable by nature. This gives us a distinct edge in the pursuit of our business interests as well. We *can* quickly adapt to changing scenarios.

Middle-class Indians are intelligent, possessing the skill of finding and making affordable purchases to substitute what may be otherwise beyond our reach. We can extend this mindset to mechanical equipment and processes as well, giving us an edge in our businesses.

As an agricultural economy, Indians are always at work, tilling, ploughing, selling. We are hard-working. I believe we have this quality in our genes and we should draw confidence from it. We are also blessed with fertile land and varied seasons that are beneficial for our businesses. We are fortunate that we have inherited a very rich culture from our ancestors/forefathers.

Finally, with regard to policy, we should rest assured. India is quickly developing and is changing for the good of all concerned. Our

BUSINESS CAN CREATE LEGACY, A JOB CANNOT

government is inclined to frame policies that favour businessmen, trade and traders, emphasizing rapid economic development for this nation. The competence of the Indian businessman has never been doubted. With support from the government and governmental agencies, businessmen will soar to new heights of success.

Neha will soon have her proud moment. Just as Neha brings a new life and a blessing into this world, a businessman too can build a business from the ground—not only for himself but also for the employment and service of many others. You too can pat your back and feel a sense of achievement once you start your business venture.

Muskuraiye aur garv kijiye, kyunki aap ek businessman hain.

2

BUILD YOUR OWN COUNTRY

A proud young man sought out the famous Greek philosopher Socrates. On finding him, he announced to Socrates, 'I come here for wisdom.'

Socrates took him to the river; they walked into the water until the water reached their chests. Socrates then asked, 'What did you want?'

The young man replied proudly, 'I seek wisdom.'

Socrates, suddenly, used his might to push the man's head below and held him there. After a few seconds, he released his hold on the young man who quickly raised his head and took a breath.

Socrates asked again, 'What do you want?'

The man replied, 'I want wisdom, Socrates.'

Socrates again pushed the man's head and held it there—a little longer this time. When allowed to move his head out of the water, the young man was gasping for breath.

Socrates asked, 'What do you want now?'

The man, taking long breaths, finally replied, 'I want air ... to breathe.'

'When your head was underwater and you were unable to breathe, could you desire anything else?' Socrates asked.

The young man replied immediately. He said, 'No! I was dying and I just wanted some air to survive.'

Socrates then told him, 'You wanted air so very badly that you were unable to think of anything else. When your urge to seek wisdom is as intense as your urge to seek a single breath of air, only then will you find wisdom.'

If you happen to be a young entrepreneur or businessman, you should take a moment to ponder upon this anecdote. Take a minute. Check-in with yourself. Are you akin to the proud young man in the story? Are you also desperate for that single 'cool tip' to make your business venture a roaring success? The young man's search for wisdom ended with a gasping breath. What about you?

There may be hundreds of ways to take your business forward and reach unscaled heights, but let me share a trade secret with you. This has worked well for many business ventures of mine.

Think about the relationship between your *business* and your *country*.

Before you read any further, let us attempt a visualization exercise. Consider the head of a government, i.e., the president or prime minister (PM) of a country (depending upon the administrative system of that country) running his or her country. Visualize every single detail, every nitty-gritty of the entire system. Visualize running the country with an efficient governance structure in place.

As far as I am concerned, I do not treat my business venture like a business. For me, my business is like a country, my very own, one I have to administer and run like its administrative head.

Let me now give you my success formula to take your business towards success and profitability. Look upon your business as if it is your own country. In this country, you have been assigned the task to govern it as its CEO (chief executive officer), efficiently and effectively. You will now need your *council of ministers,* or your hierarchy comprising management, employees and workers with clearly defined roles for each position. Every minister/officer must know their duties, responsibilities and powers well. You will also need a proper system to delegate authority and to ensure transparency. In fact, you will need well-defined SOPs (standard operating procedure) for every activity you undertake in every department. Remember, having adequate systems in place ensures smooth and trouble-free operations.

In the same way that a country needs a constitution, along with laws for governance—civil, criminal, taxation and others—your business too needs similar rules. Every rule and procedure must be available in writing for all to see. You must have suitable rewards and awards in place to keep your citizens/employees motivated. Similarly, there must be a well-defined system of punishments or adverse effects, wherever required. All these should be subject to review and amendment regularly. A country has prisons, your country/business must also have suitable 'punishment postings'. In the same way that a country has radio and television channels of its own, you must have your own communication channels within the workplace. These should be two-way channels, where communications go from top to bottom and also move from bottom to the top, as and when required.

You must decide which 'programmes' will be broadcast through your channels, what kind of 'music' forms the core of your country/ business practices. You must determine the periods and cycles well in advance. You must also ensure that feedback systems are in place, enabling you to take corrective actions whenever required.

You will need to communicate with your citizens—employees, customers, vendors, service providers, government agencies and more. You must have different templates and frequencies for different occasions and communications should vary: from happy to sad, from pleasant to curt, from a high pitch to a low pitch.

In order to motivate and push yourself, you must spell out a suitable carrot-and-stick policy for yourself, where you are aware of the prizes and surprises, punishments and forebodings, the rewards and awards that may be bestowed on you, depending upon your performance as the CEO of your country/business venture.

If you think that your job will get simpler once you have all these systems of governance in place, please correct your perception once again. Look closely at the operations of your organization. You may find some loopholes if you dig deeper. Consider the organization as you would consider the model of the country. With this framework, you may be able to fine-tune many grey areas; and in due course, this may lead to a more organized and efficient business. Just like the country! Now that these systems are in place, the struggle towards efficient governance may have become easier, but as your country/business is running, there will be surprises, problems and challenges every single day. These issues may plague you daily, whether you are running a country or a business. You cannot avoid them, but you can certainly try to handle them efficiently. You need to discover appropriate solutions to these problems and give yourself time to deal with all that may come your way.

Furthermore, in-depth research and preparedness will minimize the possible losses in the future due to these uncertainties. Remember to

EVERY ENTERPRISE SHOULD STRIVE TO EXCEED EXPECTATIONS

keep these solutions ready at hand to implement them in appropriate situations. In this manner, you can plan for a better and brighter future.

Be mentally prepared to face them. The fight will go on. These daily challenges will provide you with your daily dose of thrills and adventures. I can confidently tell you that success will come once you deal with the daily difficulties of governance. The smile on your face will be your reward for running your business as if it were your own country.

3

THE ART OF FALLING

I fell ill with polio when I was just nine months old in 1971. No vaccinations had been developed at the time. I couldn't walk until I was thirteen and would be aided by my family members and our domestic workers. Thereafter, to stand independently, I had to use calipers and crutches. This was not a simple process as calipers and crutches cannot be used without formal training.

I started working with Dr Banjari, a well-known physiotherapist, undergoing training to get used to walking using these aids. The training sessions were conducted within an approximately 2,000 square foot hall, which was duly equipped with the requisite support. Even after 30 years, I clearly remember the procedures followed with Dr Banjari. I was given ultrasound therapy to relieve the pain, paraffin wax therapy on my lower limbs, dry massage using talcum powder and treatment with a TENS (transcutaneous electrical nerve stimulation) machine for pain relief as part of our daily routine. My exercise therapy involved using an abduction ladder, weight cuffs, moving my legs in a circular motion, adding weights on the legs and moving them up and down using springs. I also learnt to use parallel bars for muscles. There was even an artificial ramp, low-rise stairs and high-rise stairs with sidebars. Here is where I learnt to walk. Just before I joined Class 9, I learnt for the first time what it means to stand on my own two legs.

I was provided with a protected environment. Detailed instructions were given and practice sessions were held here. I did many exercises, and the instructors even made me walk on spilled water safely. In case we toppled over, we were taught to sustain minimal injuries.

One day, Dr Banjari called me over and said, 'Ajay, I am sure that with just a little more practice, you will be able to walk comfortably on these calipers. However, I am going to share some special tactics with you.'

'Tactics for what, Sir?' I asked in anticipation.

'For falling. I am going to teach you the art of falling.'

His statement left me completely dumbfounded. While I was trying to comprehend what exactly he meant, Dr Banjari suddenly kicked one of my crutches, which swept me off my feet and I fell.

Dr Banjari immediately bent over to help me get up and said, 'This is what I mean. The moment your brain warns you that you are about to fall, your reflex, even within a split second, should be to quickly change your posture so that you minimize the injury or avoid it altogether.'

Friends, it's not that I have never stumbled or fallen after that session with Dr Banjari. But ever since that session, whenever I have stumbled, Dr Banjari's words have always rung in my ears. He had said, 'I cannot stop you from tripping over or from falling, but I can certainly teach you to reduce the instances wherein you lose your balance. I can teach you how to survive the fall with minimal harm. If you have not perfected the art of falling, you can break your teeth or even hurt your head.'

I have kissed the ground hundreds of times, but by the grace of God and as a result of Dr Banjari's teachings, I have never sustained a major injury. At these sessions, I also learnt that I had to walk as much as I possibly could. Dr Banjari firmly told me that if I did not walk every day, I may one day not be able to walk at all.

I learned many key life lessons during my forty days of training under Dr Banjari. But two prominent lessons remain relevant. The first lesson was that you cannot stop walking, even if you fear falling. The second lesson taught the art of falling, which helped me avoid major injury.

As infants, we have fallen so often that we probably don't even remember the worst of it. As adults, we should remember that every time we have stumbled and fallen to the ground, we have picked ourselves up and moved on. Falling is simply a part of the learning process. Every time we fall, we learn in yet another way.

This applies to failures as well. Our failures have a great deal to teach us. From our failures, we learn yet another way how things should *not* be done. The wise have said, 'There is no such thing as a failure. Every failure is just another stepping stone to success.'

Of course, you must be cautious while taking decisions in the course of your business ventures. You must exercise caution while making projections for the future or while deciding your course of action. But can anyone guarantee that everything that you plan for or predict will work out? No way. Thus, make considered decisions and don't be afraid of falling or failing.

If you get into a very safe and secure zone, there is a possibility that critical business decisions may never be taken or may get unduly delayed, resulting in the failure of your business. Sometimes, late decisions or late actions are also responsible for failure. You must calculate each and every risk to minimize injury. To calculate risk in business, some popular and proven methods are available, which mainly include SWOT (strengths, weaknesses, opportunities, and threats) analysis, root cause analysis, risk register, probability and impact matrix, assumption analysis, etc. Additionally, you may take the advice of an experienced team of consultants. You can also refer to similar case studies for greater insight into the matter. In order to mitigate risk, you can also be insured. It is far better to be prepared with an alternative plan of action, in case you fail/fall. Often, failing or falling makes you wiser and this will assist you in future.

For example, injury is commonly sustained by cricketers and parkour artists. However, incidents of serious injury are not as common. Both parkour artists as well as cricketers are taught techniques to maintain their balance and to manage the momentum of their fall. They can channel their falls and spring back into action. The trick is to try and convert the probable long-term injuries into short-term pain or injury. The same can be applied to your business.

In your business, learn to fall in a manner where you either minimize the injury or damage or not fail at all. Master the art of falling in life, and in business as well. In the footsteps of Dr Banjari, I would like to give you an important tip.

No matter how many times you fall, it is essential that you do not sustain a serious injury.

RISE AGAIN

4

GET RID OF THE SIDE SUPPORTS

My neighbours and friends, Sonal and Ashish Singhal live across the street with their twins. Of the two sons, the younger, Aarush, is more proactive, demanding and somewhat dominating. His slightly older twin, Aarav, is less naughty and prefers to follow in the footsteps of his brother. Whether purchasing a toy, a book or even a balloon, Mr Singhal has to buy two of each item to avoid a quarrel between the two.

One day, I noticed Mr Singhal bringing in two small bicycles with side supports—one red and one yellow—for his twin sons. A few days later, I saw that Aarush had already begun to ride his bicycle without the side supports. He was giddily waving at Aarav and his proud father, who were both cheering him on. Aarav clutched his father's hand tightly.

I went over and asked Aarav where his bicycle was and why he was not riding with his brother. Before the young boy could reply,

Mr Singhal spoke up. 'You see, it's my fault. Both of them started learning cycling at the same time, but Aarav cannot balance himself on his bicycle. He fell off his bicycle a few days ago and lost all his confidence. He says that he does not enjoy riding his bicycle any more. He is scared to fall off and injure himself.'

'But how are you responsible for this?' I asked.

'Out of concern for Aarav,' he said. 'I allowed him to ride his bicycle with the side supports on for a long time. I wanted him to be confident that he could maintain his balance by practising enough with the side supports. When I finally removed the side supports, he couldn't balance himself beyond a certain distance.'

'But you must have taught Aarush the same way?'

Mr Singhal shook his head.

'I removed one of the two side supports after seven days of practice by Aarush. When I saw that he was riding the bicycle confidently with one side support, I removed the other. All this happened in less than two weeks. But in Aarav's case, I removed both the side supports at once.' Saying this, Mr Singhal sighed and continued, 'I think I made two mistakes. One, I left both the side supports on for a long time for Aarav, much longer than was actually required. And second, I removed both the side supports at the same time, instead of removing them gradually.'

Later, at home, I thought about this peculiar situation. I realized that Aarav had gotten used to riding his bicycle with the side supports on for too long. In the beginning, Aarush cycled with both side supports and enjoyed his cycling routine. Over the course of many such training days, one side support was removed from his cycle intentionally. This meant that Aarush still had an arrangement he could fall back on if he were to feel like he was falling. After two to three days, the second side support was also removed to verify how Aarush responded to the change. Surprisingly, Aarush gained confidence and learnt to balance himself gradually.

Simultaneously removing them both led to his many falls. And now, he had no confidence and had accepted his failure. In Aarush's case, the change was slower. Aarush was able to confidently ride, relying on both, then one single side support. I thought this situation could be applied to the business world as well.

In business, as in training bicycles, some key supports are always present, right from its inception. These permanent supports are perpetual. In addition to permanent supports, many side or temporary supports exist as well, these must be removed gradually, soon after the business has set off. You must make a list of all your temporary support systems and remove them gradually, one at a time.

The support received from the government and agencies is temporary. The special incentives and benefits, the tax-free zones or special economic zones (SEZs) are governmental aids to promote businesses and provide a conducive environment for exports. This advantage is not a perpetual one and a business needs to strategize keeping this in mind.

If your business idea is unique, the initial competition may be low but in the long run, this will quickly change. Similarly, geographical advantages available in certain areas can also only be availed of within a limited duration. Businessmen are provided with capital for their business at reduced rates of interest, but this is available only in certain cases and only within certain fixed terms. Likewise, the availability of free/affordable power to businesses is a limited benefit from the government to encourage growth in potential segments. Sometimes, you may find cheap labour but this will not last forever. You may

INDEPENDENCE IS AN ART TO BE MASTERED

initially enjoy the benefits of research and development (R&D) in all domains, but they are only available for a fixed tenure. Several benefits of economic reforms may be reaped for a short while before the policies change.

Having identified these support systems, you must draw a time-bound plan to remove each of the supports that benefit your business. Pay attention to two particular situations and avoid them. First, removing these supports prematurely will be detrimental to your business. Second, allowing side support to linger long after its utility will also result in a negative situation.

It is important to note that these situations will vary from case to case, and utmost caution must be exercised while identifying and removing your supports. The long- and short-term impact of continuing to use these supports should be mapped and studied. The effect of their removal should be studied well in advance as well, keeping in mind the sustainability and profitability of your business as well as the impact on your brand identity.

Strike a balance in your business by managing both your permanent and temporary support systems.

5

ONE PAIR OF DENTURES

An elderly couple in their late seventies frequented a popular fast-food restaurant located at the corner of their street. The joint was known for its delicious foot-long paper masala dosa, served with piping hot sambhar and four different kinds of chutneys.

The couple usually occupied the table facing the window and ordered their favourite paper masala dosa, chatting like old friends until their order was served on their table. They giggled like a young couple out on their very first date.

The woman would cut a small portion with her knife, scoop it up and dip it in one of the chutneys and sambhar and lovingly feed her doting husband until the plate was empty. Once the first paper masala dosa was over, they would order another plate for themselves. This time, the husband would follow the same script. He would dip the bite-sized piece first in the chutney and then in the sambhar and would gently put it in his wife's mouth. The restaurant staff and the other regulars noticed the couple, week after week, staring in awe as the couple treated each other with love, care and patience. Sometimes the onlookers wondered why the couple would not order two dosas simultaneously.

One day, a curious waiter approached the elderly couple and remarked, 'I admire the love, perseverance and care that both of you have for each other. But one thing has been bothering me a little.'

The elderly gentleman asked, 'And what exactly is that, young man?'

The waiter continued, 'Sir, I have observed that every time, you order just one plate of paper masala dosa, finish your meal and only then do you order another plate for madam. Why is it that you don't order two plates of masala dosa and eat the dish together?'

The old man could not hide his amusement. He replied with a smile, 'Oh, that's simple. It is because, between the two of us, we only have a single pair of dentures. When I am eating, my wife patiently waits for her turn. Similarly, if she is eating first, I wait for my turn.'

With this, the couple and the onlooker all burst into laughter.

Do you, like the adoring couple, also run your business on a single set of dentures?

In the restaurant, once everyone recovered from the hearty laughter, the young waiter stood still and perplexed.

He asked, 'But uncle, why don't you buy another pair of dentures?'

The elderly lady replied, 'Son, we can. But we are worried about two things. What if the fit of the dentures is not right? And worse, what if the new pair is better than our existing one? Then both of us may fight for the new pair of dentures. And since we have decided not to fight or disagree in our old age, we discarded the idea of buying a new pair of dentures.'

In the same way, your business may be successful today but what if you are affected adversely in your domain? If your dentures are fractured or if they crack, it may become difficult for you to make ends meet. It may result in a fight. But our businesses are not like dentures, and we need more than one to survive in a world of competition.

Prudent businessmen have more than one line of business just in case. What if one business faces hiccups? There the other parallel businesses will recover the losses. Even if one business bleeds to death and bankruptcy, the other businesses will keep the ball rolling.

If you are running your business on a single model, the chances are that it may become obsolete one day. You need to diversify your business. Study the consumption and behavioural patterns of customers and it will be easy to ideate new businesses and start working on a suitable project.

In India, the education sector is still a green sector. When I established myself in the field, I decided to take a leap forward. I began to move into the university segment. Even at Bachpan, I began a furniture manufacturing unit. The unit not only manufactures furniture for our playschools and formal schools but also specializes in manufacturing complete home furniture and is available in the market. Similarly, to keep up quality control and follow best practices, we started our uniform factory years ago. Growing gradually, this unit has now transformed into a full-fledged garment manufacturing unit.

You have to build your strengths to improve/build your business portfolio. Be alert about economic changes, government policies and procedures, competition, global perspective and availability of resources. Think like an organization that has an existing business line and is looking to diversify. This can be done either by re-engineering your existing ecosystem or fine-tuning it a little bit. Think like an entrepreneur who doesn't have a full-fledged ecosystem in place. Think about reengineering your business from the beginning and think about venturing into new businesses. You can think like an investor who eagerly explores and identifies new segments for foreign direct investment (FDI) options. Thus, the options with investors are multifold and yet untapped. Many versatile concepts are emerging every day and must be explored. Hence, one pair of dentures shouldn't be relied upon. Instead, choose to have multiple pairs of dentures.

Consider what you can do to expand. Personally, I too contemplated what else/what more we could do to expand with our existing resources and infrastructure. This led me to add healthcare to my business portifolio after education. Just like education, healthcare also happens to be a greenfield sector. I wanted to get deeper into the healthcare sector but in a calibrated manner. Therefore, I opted for the gateway to healthcare and started a diagnostic centre under the name of 'Must & More'.

I firmly believe that you must not only have multiple pairs of dentures but also have multiple jaws. Single dentures may be good for marriages, but multiple arrangements are necessary to lead your business to long-term success.

EXPAND OR PERISH

6

RISKPRENEUR

Once upon a time, there was a fisherman who would row out on his boat, travelling several miles far into the ocean. Only then would he cast his net. He always hoped for a big catch. Whether the sea was calm and serene or very turbulent, he remained unperturbed. Every morning, he would wake up at the crack of dawn and steer his boat to the middle of the ocean. He would return home in the evening, a big catch slung over his shoulder every single day. That was how he made a living for himself and his family.

One day, a close friend of the fisherman asked, 'Every day you go out into the deep sea, braving turbulent tides. Don't you feel scared?'

The fisherman shook his head.

'Remember, your father died while casting a net in rough waters. Why don't you give up this profession and do something else for a living?'

The fisherman smiled before replying.

'My dear friend, your mother died in her sleep. Have you given up sleeping since then?'

Some prefer waiting by the sea, waiting for the tide to turn favourable. Others prefer to drop the fishing rod into the water while relaxing in a bamboo chair. Some people dare to swim through deep and strong currents to fish. Others prefer to swim close to the shore where the water runs shallow. Yet some others simply prefer to dip their toes at the seashore. To each his own.

In other words, every individual has his own comfort zone. Humans are generally reluctant to move out of their comfort zones. We don't want to explore bigger opportunities; we happily settle for whatever is available and within our reach. When I glance around, I find that a large number of people are content to simply sit at the seashore, watching the tides.

I don't think that anyone should immediately jump into the deep end of the sea! But I also don't believe that big fish can be caught by fishing along the seashore. To land a big fish, you will have to go deeper.

Yes, it is absolutely true that no business can be undertaken without risk. Whenever I talk about risk, it does not imply a blind rush into risky ventures. Instead, risks must be reasonably taken when the losses can be borne. The risk must be well calculated in business. No risk, no gain, they say, and it is true.

Simply put, you cannot make a profit unless you take a risk—whether in terms of money due to defaulted payments, theft, increase in the cost of operations, loss in investments or anything else. Some business projects demand all your time and effort, which can also be a risk. Further, almost every opportunity comes with a risk, even something like losing your social status or becoming unpopular amongst your friends and relatives. It is critically important to assess all the risks associated with any business activity before starting a new venture.

Once you become aware that the survival of your business depends on your measured or calculated risks, it is imperative to conduct a risk–reward analysis for every single activity. As a rule, the risk to reward ratio must always be taken into consideration. Or we can say that the anticipated rewards should be well above the quantum of risk that you would be taking. Further, the quantum of risk should be well within your risk-taking capacity. In other words, you should only bite as much as you can chew. While conducting a business, you have to write down all the risks and their potential outcomes in terms of profits, losses and uncertainties. The reasons must be thoroughly analysed before proceeding any further. These studies can become guides in the uncertain future as well.

It is well established that as you age, your risk-taking capability decreases. When you are young and starting a new business, you can afford to take big risks. As you grow old, you tend to look for relatively safer pastures. The risk here is limited and the returns are as well. In life, when you begin your business ventures you are likely to be a bachelor with little to no liability; you can afford to take big risks, financial or otherwise. As the size of your family grows and you have more and more liabilities, your tendency to take risks also reduces. It is always advisable to move with the times and settle for commensurate returns, which could be low in certain cases.

However, even seasoned businessmen grow too cautious and fearful. They avoid taking any risks at all. Without knowing it, they move from the risk zone to the fear zone, which is bad for business. They tend to lose their risk-taking capability and become apprehensive. This tendency could soon become a part of their very nature. Such a situation needs to be identified and corrected at the earliest. If this is not done, it may be detrimental to your business and your profits may dwindle soon after.

If you rely only on calculations done in your mind, I strongly believe

THERE IS A MADMAN INSIDE EVERY ENTREPRENEUR

that it is now time to change this practice. It is always worthwhile to maintain an Excel sheet and thoughtfully record the risks, gains against the risks and your Plan B, in case your Plan A fails. Mention these in columns for ready reference and quick implementation.

One important piece of advice I have to share is that whenever you are taking such strategic decisions, ensure that the deciding factors are well documented on the Excel sheet by you or your team. Always revisit the points before implementation. This preparedness will also help you to brainstorm the decisions taken and help in evaluating their effectiveness in the future.

Finally, it is my opinion that aspiring businessmen should take the risk and start a new business. Existing businessmen should continue to take small and measured risks on an ongoing basis. To expand any business, risks will have to be taken.

Remember, opportunities and the sea are both wide-open for everyone to explore and take advantage of. But safety and survival are also equally important. So dive into the ocean. Have all your safety gear in place. Best of luck!

7

SEEMA KE PAKODE

Seema Sharma, the wife of my close friend, is not only an expert cook but also an ever-smiling hostess. Whenever our group of friends visits her house, she is ever-willing to serve varied and delicious snacks whipped up in her kitchen. She makes them while we chat over sundry matters and spend our time gossiping. Of all the snacks that she prepares, her vegetable pakodas merit a special mention.

Seema is overjoyed and exuberant and we shower her with praises. However, Seema's husband has a contrary opinion. He believes that while Seema is good at home-cooking, there is nothing extraordinary about her culinary skills.

Whatever his opinion may be, the fact is that all of us enjoy eating pakodas at her house, particularly on a rainy or cold day. On one such day, after enjoying a variety of pakodas, one of us commented, 'Seema bhabhi, you cook such delectable pakodas that I suggest that you open a pakoda shop. Your shop will soon be a hit. Not only in our neighbourhood, but in the entire city. Trust me, you will become very popular in no time.'

My friend, our host, did not appreciate this friendly comment and said, 'If you guys had it your way you will soon instigate her into opening a shop, naming it Seema ke pakode. Cooking pakodas for a handful of people does not mean that she can cook them for masses, or even that they will all like it. She does not have the skills required to do such a thing at a professional level. To conduct a business on such a scale, you need a proper shop, skilled and trained manpower, regular supply of raw material, utensils like a large kadhai, crockery, big burners, storage and sitting space, bank accounts and so much more. Moreover, I have never heard of or seen a lady in such a business. And in any case, everyone in our family has a job. We do not have any background in business operations. Seema is well educated and qualified. She definitely deserves much more than a mere pakoda shop.'

We tried to encourage our friend by giving him examples of several such successful ventures. His expressions denoted acceptance, but he did not pay heed to it.

We found ourselves in a peculiarly helpless situation. Seema too could neither agree with her husband nor could she readily express her disagreement. We politely wound up the discussion and left for our homes. This incident was soon forgotten.

This incident took place around two years ago.

However, today Mrs Seema Sharma earns close to two lakh rupees per month from her pakoda shop. Although it is not a shop. Seema instead has been running a cookery show on YouTube. The first recipe she shared was of our favourite pakodas. Seema has crossed the 500-subscriber mark for her episodes, and her most popular recipe remains those pakodas. Today, Seema's daughter has also started her independent channel on YouTube where she specializes in baking cakes and savouries. When I spoke with Seema, she told me that the seed for this novel initiative was sown for the first time when we recommended that she start a pakoda shop. She said, 'Somehow, the idea of transforming my passion and interest into a business and earning model took root in me and touched my heart. Since then, I started looking for different ways to get started. Finally, the dream took some shape with the start of a successful cookery show on YouTube.'

I must congratulate Seema for her success and persistence!

With the advent of the Internet, innumerable new ideas and opportunities have opened up for business. Enterprising entrepreneurs are starting new businesses every single day. No shops or trading licences are required to start these businesses. Nor are any signboards, employees and premises mandatory for operating the business. Gone are the dependencies on conventional ways of finding your customer and client base. These businesses range from groceries to education and include everything under the sun. The number of prospective customers could well run into lakhs and crores.

All that a new-age business needs is a smartphone with an internet connection and a smattering of confidence. With just these technologies, you can now cater to a vast majority of the country's population.

It is likely that you too have unique qualities and interests that you can exploit. It could be making delicious pakodas or multicuisine dishes or baking your favourite cakes and cookies. Your love for gardening can encourage you to start online sessions on gardening knowledge and growing organic vegetables too. Your interest in teaching can make you an online schoolteacher for kids or even a tuition teacher as per your specialization and qualification. Your enthusiasm to travel across the entire world can make you a blogger, organizer, consultant and help you earn within the field of adventure. Your ability to write and speak can open the door to endless possibilities from being an author, editor, content creator, speaker, trainer and a lot more. You can teach any art form, from mandala to Madhubani to calligraphy and much more. If you are a versatile dancer, you can take inspiration from the late Saroj Khan, who taught dance on television or the graceful Madhuri Dixit (who too teaches dancing online). Similarly, if you are good at vocal or instrumental music, you will find learners across the globe. You can sell apparel, jewellery or handcrafted material online. You can give consultation from your home for interior decoration, health and wellness.

This is an opportune time for you to explore the potential to make your skill or hobby reach lakhs of people. In this process, you could also be a big beneficiary, in monetary terms and otherwise. Online selling has already found its place in our lives. The number of businesses and businessmen are increasing at a fast pace every day. Small products, including those made at home or by individual craftsmen, are finding a ready market due to online commerce. This is true for the service sector as well.

You need not have any apprehensions regarding the scope of selling your products or services, irrespective of their size or the quantum of production.

Look at the market. Let the product or service be judged by the open market. Let the demand in the market determine the future of your products or services. Believe me, market forces are much smarter than you and I. They are not only smarter but also more versatile. Today digitization has made the advertisement and marketing of your business affordable and accessible. You don't have to plan and allot huge budgets as the packages are quite pocket-friendly and customized

FROM THOUGHTSMITH TO DOER

by service providers for different users. You just need to explore the options based on your needs and the size of your business. These efforts will help you increase your chances of success.

In the meantime, I am eagerly awaiting the day I can place an online order with Seema ke pakode to be delivered steaming hot through a service. Today, I am certain that Sharmaji is proud of Seema and willing to finance Seema bhabhi's cloud kitchen.

Endless possibilities are knocking at your door. Keep your options open and choose the best of them.

8

THEREFORE

A young man had just completed his postgraduation. Having received good grades, he was now in search of an appropriate job. The local member of the legislative assembly (MLA) lived in his neighbourhood. And so, one day, the boy approached the MLA and requested that he recommend his case to the chief minister (CM). The MLA agreed. The young man would be escorted to visit the CM for a personal interview the very next day.

That day, the boy returned to the MLA's office, ready with his certificates and his degree and together they left for the CM's office.

However, the MLA soon realized that a stench emanated from the young man. He questioned him. The young man replied abashedly that his socks always carried a stink; he was tired of it, but nothing could be done about it. The MLA immediately reprimanded him and told him that they couldn't see the CM in such a state. He sent the man home and asked him to return the next day, wearing fresh socks.

The following day, the young man returned to the MLA's office and they set off. Within a few moments, the MLA realized that the stench remained.

He shouted, 'I told you to change your socks! What's wrong with you?'

The man replied immediately, 'Sir, I bought a new pair of socks and am wearing them. I knew that you would not believe me, therefore, I have brought with me the receipt for my new pair.'

This particular adverb, 'therefore', is the theme of this chapter. The adverb plays a rather critical role in an entrepreneur's journey. Our success stories as well as the stories of our failures begin with and end with this single word—therefore.

Let us go back in time and look at two episodes from our history which will emphasize the power of 'therefore' or 'because of' in our lives. One about the origin of the Ramayana, and the other regarding the battle recounted in the Mahabharat.

Perhaps you are aware that the renowned poet Goswami Tulsidas was once just an ordinary man, enamoured with his beloved. When his newly wedded wife went to visit her parents, Goswami Tulsidas followed her there. Upon seeing him at her maternal home, his wife was astounded and annoyed. She openly reprimanded him for his behaviour. Therefore, from this point the world received the blessings of the lord, the supreme creator of this universe in the form of the Ramayana. If not for the timely reprimand, we would not have had such a work.

Similarly, the battle of Mahabharata would not have been fought had Shakuni not objected when five villages had to be granted to the Pandavas by the Kauravas, in line with the proposal for peace brought by Lord Krishna. The Pandavas would have quietly agreed to a small share of their kingdom and a battle that claimed countless lives would have never been fought. Though the battle lines had clearly been drawn between the Kauravas and the Pandavas, Arjuna decided otherwise. He laid down his bow and arrow and told Lord Krishna that he did not want to fight against his own clan.

The tale is famous. Arjuna told Lord Krishna that he had clarity, that even if the Pandavas won this battle, it would be futile; without their near and dear ones, they wouldn't be able to live happily in their kingdom.

Therefore, when Arjuna laid his weapons down and lost his will to fight, Lord Krishna delivered the holy sermon, which we now know as the Bhagavad Gita. This revered sermon is regarded as scripture by all. The universal messages that it contains answer the deepest questions concerning life and death. Had Arjuna not stopped in the battlefield, the situation would have been different.

Similarly, whether you are looking at your life or your business, you will find that there is a huge difference between what comes before a decision or an important event—the 'pre- therefore' and the 'post- therefore'. Invariably, the 'post- therefore' events have been unpredictable and unthinkable, both in terms of their direction as well as their magnitude. Either you will be an example to be quoted as a symbol of success or you will remain as a symbol of one who made the wrong analysis of the 'pre- therefore'. There is a very important hidden message here. Can you see it?

In business, there are many such moments. Sometimes, we are able to identify these moments. By taking immediate action, often reflexively, we turn the tables in our favour. We achieve phenomenal results. Our business, thereafter, takes a different direction and moves at an unprecedented pace, resulting in increased profitability and growth. However, on many occasions, we are too involved with the daily activities of our business and we miss out.

Not many businessmen had predicted the results of online payments. Few of us had seen the magnitude of change that would come about once chequebooks, pen drives, telegrams, demand drafts, landline phones had been rendered meaningless through new technology. 'Therefore' is a magical word. 'Therefore' can have a negative connotation and a negative impact. But noticing the consequences of an event can also yield great rewards.

If you can see these moments, you may also see the risk attached to them. You can choose to capitalize on a 'therefore moment' or you can let it go. You can opt to forget a 'therefore' moment; you can also remember it to implement it in the future.

Furthermore, your personal 'therefore' moments may be quite different from a 'therefore' in the open market. You will find that 'therefore' is a double-edged sword. You should be careful while choosing *your* particular situation. The need of the hour is to be on the prowl and identify these moments.

DON'T HIDE BEHIND EXCUSES

9

A NOVEL IDEA

Are you looking for a novel business idea? Something unprecedented, like the Ola and Uber ideas, like Swiggy, Zomato or Byju's? Many of my friends in business have been on the prowl for new concepts, often referred to as virgin business ideas, for years. None of them have been able to find something so grand.

I want to share a detail that may give insight and perspective, but before I do so, let me share a story about the legendary film producer and the late director Yash Chopra. Yash Chopra has always been popular; he has ruled the hearts of Bollywood film buffs for many decades. He had a knack for telling love stories in many imaginative ways. He did it well enough to keep his audiences, young and old alike, glued to their seats.

In 1970, Yash Chopra started his own production house, Yash Raj Films. Soon after, he invited five or six writers to his office to discuss their long-term plan of action. He announced that he had already finalized the themes and the genre for the films he would go on to make in the next two decades. He gave each of them an opportunity: if the story any of them wrote met the standards set by the production house, the writer would get to write the screenplay and the dialogues for the film. The chosen writer would have a long-term contract with Yash Raj Films.

The writers were overjoyed at the prospect. They quickly brought out their pens and their notebooks.

Yash Chopra announced, 'My first film will be a love story. My second film too will be a love story. My third film will be a love story. My fourth, fifth and all subsequent films will also be love stories. Please start working on your stories immediately and submit them. Each story should be different from the others.'

This decision left the writers baffled. They couldn't figure out why a seasoned film director and producer would stick to old style. Why was he not inclined to experiment with some new-age themes, some experimental ideas and unique storylines, they wondered?

Yash Chopra firmly believed that he would work on something that he knew best; he would not deviate from his favourite theme of romance and love.

He was aware that it was impossible for him to develop too many novel ideas. He also knew that experimentation brought with it inherent risks. And he knew that he was passionate about making films based on romantic love stories. Beginning in the 1970s, Yash Chopra made a series of films, all of them successes: *Kabhi Kabhie, Silsila, Chandni, Lamhe, Dilwale Dulhaniya Le Jayenge, Dil Toh Pagal Hai, Mohabbatein, Veer Zara, Rab Ne Bana Di Jodi, Jab Tak Hai Jaan.* They were all love stories. They were all superhits. He won six national film awards and eight Filmfare Awards. In 2001, he won the Dada Saheb Phalke Award and in 2005, he was awarded the Padma Bhushan. In 2006, Yash Chopra was awarded Lifetime Membership of the British Academy of Film & Television Arts (BAFTA). Remember, all the films that contributed to his roaring success were based only on love stories.

You can learn an important lesson from this.

Instead of wasting your time looking and waiting for a novel idea to kick-start your business, it is better to draw upon an already existing idea and tradition. It should just meet two criteria: first, the business idea that you pick must be to your liking and ideally, you should be passionate about it; second, you must have some expertise in the field that you choose from, conversant with and confident that you can take the idea forward to its logical conclusion.

The story narrated above is based on my imagination. It is a tribute to Yash Chopra, who succeeded in becoming a legend. I wanted to drive home the point that Yash Chopra used the 'same old theme' of a love story. Similarly, you too can find an already existing business idea that meets the two criteria and start your journey.

However, it must be said that many other love stories have been filmed, even after the demise of Yash Chopra. But not all these films have found success at the box office. The strength and USP (unique selling proposition) of each and every Yash Chopra film was the way each story was told, how it was carried forward from frame to frame. This vision must be developed as you begin your business. Certain factors can help towards this vision; you may strategize and bend your efforts to stand out from the crowd. Consider a scenario wherein existing businesses have been mastered by you to a good extent. Every business is connected to various dimensions and, if looked at carefully, they can be your next business opportunity. Moreover, if you are able to decode the possibilities even in any one particular dimension, then the chances of being successful will be greater in comparison to ventures initiated

REINVENTION IS THE ALGORITHM OF SUCCESS

with a virgin idea.

As the leader, make sure to elaborate on your conceptualization of the basic business idea. Your team can do the detailed research but you must do the homework in terms of a feasibility study with due emphasis on the returns on capital. You may even need to work on the break-even point and wait through the gestation period. Furthermore, you must plan the presentation and packaging of the business concept in an innovative way. Your marketing methods, techniques and your attitude towards the business and its various components will decide its fate.

The most important thing is to establish a connection within the business as well as with the market. Don't forget the SWOT analysis for your business, products and your clients. Don't forget to identify the USP of your product or service. Don't forget to make detailed plans.

Please don't wait for your virgin idea. Pick up a business passion and get going. Remember, you are only getting older with each passing day.

10

MAGGI-INSPIRED BUSINESS

Three years ago, my aunt, Usha Gupta, was intent on finding a suitable match for her son, Rahul, a handsome and accomplished boy. Like many other aspiring men, Rahul had some expectations and he shared these with his mother. He wanted to marry a beautiful woman. He wanted her to be tall, educated, fair and from a respectable family. Rahul was very particular that his wife must be an excellent cook.

She must have a passion for cooking and trying out new dishes, Rahul had said. My aunt herself is a brilliant cook and is interested in serving the best dishes to her beloved family.

During the long-drawn-out process of matchmaking, my aunt met a beautiful and accomplished girl who ticked all the right boxes. She enthusiastically asked, 'Are you fond of cooking?'

The girl nodded politely.

My aunt continued. 'What are the dishes that you can cook? And what is it that you really enjoy cooking?'

My aunt was surprised by her reply.

The girl proudly said, 'I am an expert at cooking Maggi. I make a number of variations and they are all very delicious. None of my friends or family members can cook Maggi in as many different ways and combinations as I do.'

I don't think that I need to tell you whether this matchmaking exercise was fruitful or not. You can well imagine the outcome.

Do you know that any Maggi-inspired business is the best business for India? If your business is inspired by Maggi, then it will be an early success and a profitable one. You may disagree but read on. Maggi has something to teach every businessman.

Maggi is a distinctive product. If your product can be designed distinctively, then success is likely to follow. If your products and services are unique, clients are likely to pay the price you quote as well. If you observe closely, you will find that Maggi occupies a unique space in the minds of Indian people and in Indian kitchens, schools, colleges, hostels, bachelor dens, college canteens and on all the shelves of big and small stores and huge departmental stores. If your business can cater to as many different sets of clients as Maggi, though they may be based in other localities, towns, cities or states, you will succeed. To do this you will need to know exactly how you want to scale up your business: online or offline. You must plan a robust distribution mechanism in terms of network and strategies. Many businesses today are producing goods and services for every generation with innovative strategies that enable them to be the first choice of every buyer.

Maggi is a food item. Hence the manufacturers have focused on the richness of its taste and its consistency. It was thus accepted by a large population despite varied taste buds. Similarly, you must focus on the richness of your products, services and business as a whole. This is achievable when you make the effort to improve your product's features and the experience of customers. Remember that consistency is key here.

Maggi is recognized as an established Indian brand and valued for its success. With time, Maggi has been successful in building a client base that supports it wholeheartedly. We must similarly win the trust and confidence of our clients and customers to become a brand.

To become a brand, you must build a rapport with your business and the end user over a period of time. Your business should not have a casual approach while dealing with customers. You become a brand when you behave like a brand.

Another interesting feature of Maggi, as evidenced by my aunt's experience, is that it goes well with other ingredients and it still tastes just as good. Maggi is distinctive but it doesn't have an ego. Similarly, we must also watch our businesses and ask ourselves—does it have an element of acceptability and adaptability? Are we open to bringing in other products and services that complement our existing products and services? Are we ready to blend, modify and innovate our existing products and services to increase their acceptance and demand in the market? This will enhance customer experience and boost sales. In a business, if innovation is not accepted and encouraged, the potential for growth will be limited.

Maggi has a unique quality of adaptability. It may transform its shape depending on use, but it doesn't lose its originality. Your business too must ensure a quality check of its products and services for the end user. Again, this helps in building trust and confidence among buyers. You get word-of-mouth publicity and referrals in your business without any effort on your part. You may increase your operations but remember that quality checks must be followed on a regular basis.

Maggi is eaten as a full meal, as a part of snacks and even as a filler. Similarly, businesses should think about fulfilling their clients' needs and expectations in all ways. It is important to know what a buyer wants while delivering variety for the customer. If you are successful in doing this homework, you will be able to modify the quantum and usability for every user. You will create a new range for first-time users as well. Make it part of the process. Check the tastes and preferences of your customers along with market trends to meet clients' expectations.

Maggi is affordable and suits every pocket. Similarly, you must work on the price effectiveness of your products and services. Yes, inflation and market trends may at times guide you to increase the prices of products and services, but you must be reasonable about it.

Maggi's personality is such that it works as an all-time food. Similarly, if you are in the consumer business, then your products should also be all-time products.

Consider these advantages.

Maggi has great customer care. I once read that a businessman must always sleep with his boots on. You too must be ready to handle business situations with patience round the clock. With a positive attitude, you should even be ready to attend to customer complaints at odd hours. You must take immediate corrective actions as far as possible.

As a businessman, you must learn another important lesson from Maggi. You must have innumerable friends. If you have only two friends, then in times of need your options will be limited. Nowadays, we relate the characteristics of this product with the traits of a businessman. The benchmarks set by Maggi boast of an intelligently packed product that has created a tradition of winning the trust of its customers. It

#INSPIRATION IS EVERYWHERE, LOOK INTENTLY

has secured its place, especially in Indian households, becoming the smallest reason for everyone's happiness.

Much earlier, it was not an easy task for Maggi to penetrate into the Indian market. But with their holistic approach and multidimensional focus points, it has become one of the greatest case studies for any businessman to refer to and learn from.

Be a Maggi-inspired personality and try to be popular enough to call the masses your friends.

11

BE A LION, BE A BUSINESSMAN

Once upon a time, there was a poor woodcutter who lived in a village near the jungle. He lived a happy life in his village with his wife, two small children and a pet goat. They loved the pet goat. Every day, the children played joyfully with the goat. And every day, their father, the woodcutter, would head into the jungle and chop some trees. He sold the timber for living and used the left over wood fuel to cook food.

One cold evening, while returning from the jungle, the woodcutter chanced upon a strange sight. He saw a newborn lion cub alone and unattended. He stood at a distance, curiously gazing at the cub, waiting for the lioness or the lion.

He was afraid to pick up the cub despite its whimpers, fearing the wrath of the lioness.

After a while, he finally decided to leave the cub and went home.

He narrated this unusual incident to his wife. His wife said that it was indeed a peculiar situation. But the cub would surely die of the chill in the air if left unattended, she opined. They could not be so unkind to a poor lion cub.

The woodcutter and his wife decided to return to the spot to look for the whimpering lion cub. On seeing the shivering cub in the same spot, they took pity and brought the baby home. With the addition of the lion cub, the farmer's family now had six members in all.

The poor man, his wife and two children enjoyed living and playing with the goat and the lion cub every day thereafter. The lion cub grew close to the goat and they became great friends, the younger cub often imitating the older goat. Two years passed.

The lion cub was playful, but in conduct and behaviour, the lion now resembled the goat. It did not have the fierce qualities generally associated with predators. Seeing this, the man's neighbours often told him that he was domesticating a lion cub into a docile goat. They felt that the cub would never be able to grow up and be a lion, as was his nature. They told him to go and leave the cub in the jungle so that the cub could grow in its natural habitat.

With a heavy heart and much against the wishes of the children, the couple decided to take the lion cub and leave it in the jungle. The wife insisted that they watch from a distance till the lion disappeared into the dense growth. But that was not to be. As soon as they released the lion cub and it started heading away from them, a pack of wild dogs attacked the lion and killed it. The lion cub was so weak and meek that it could not defend itself. It had no ability to fight and kill the stray jungle dogs as these qualities had never been taught to it. Having lived with the goat for two years, captive and deprived of natural training, had made the lion cub meek.

Here is an important business lesson. In order to survive and thrive in any business, I have to be a lion to be a businessman. I cannot afford to have a soft and compromising approach, much like the goat, while engaging in business.

A lion cub must learn the laws of the jungle to live and fight independently; a businessman too has to be aggressive and dynamic in order to survive and prosper in this highly competitive world. He has to fight his own battles, every day.

If your competitors adopt fiercely competitive marketing strategies, your mild marketing activities will not aid you. If they opt for innovative digital marketing practices, you cannot confine your marketing activities to conventional marketing styles. And this rule applies to all the functions—your competitors may constantly be improving their product quality or adding innovative features to their products at frequent intervals of time, while you lag behind.

You will have to be proactive. You must increase your social media presence if your competitor has a sizeable presence across all media channels. If your competitor takes initiatives towards providing employee satisfaction, your business must do better. If your competitor is intolerant of substandard quality products, then you too must focus on achieving consistency in quality and have regular quality checks in place. If your competitor emphasizes customer satisfaction, don't forget to improve on customer feedback processes in your business and ensure good after-sales service.

Be up to date on the quality of the packaging of your competitors and try to match their superior quality. Remember to streamline the operations of your production, marketing and payment collection divisions to stay in tune with the best practices followed by your competitors. You have to take the lead in a process-based approach as well as other departments, such as raw material procurement. You will have to be one step ahead of your competitors in every possible way.

Like a lion and a businessman, you will imbibe the qualities of a lion in the jungle. Be fierce, firm, ruthless, aggressive and dynamic. If you choose to be a goat, then the lions and even the wild dogs amongst your competitors will kill your business.

In today's fast changing world, you have to be the predator that knows no limits or boundaries. That is your way to success. May you rule the jungle.

FEROCITY GIVES VELOCITY

12

WHAT KIND OF A BUSINESSMAN ARE YOU?

On a leisurely day, I conducted three simple experiments at home.

For the first, I took an egg. It was fragile and would have broken as soon as it dropped to the floor. The liquid egg white and the yellow yolk would have spilled on to the floor. But the thin and hard outer shell safely held the embryo inside it. I boiled this egg for eight minutes. The contents inside the egg had now taken a solid form. However, the colour of the water it had been boiled in had not changed at all.

Next, I took a raw potato, which is hard by nature, and placed it inside a pressure cooker with water and cooked it for ten minutes. When I took it out, it had become soft and pliable. In this case, the water had not changed in colour either.

Next, I put some roasted coffee beans in a pot of water and boiled them. The coffee beans had a different impact on the water. The colour of the water soon changed to a dark brown and a magical aroma emanated from the coffee grounds. This aroma was an indication that the coffee was ready for consumption.

Although my experiments and their results were simple, even expected, it forced me to put on my thinking cap. In all three cases, water was boiled and the egg, the potato and the ground coffee beans were impacted by the boiling heat. When we boiled the egg and potato, the attributes of the water did not change. But the coffee beans had an altogether different effect on the water.

Let us look at human behaviour in the light of the above details. If three individuals happen to face the same adverse situation or adversity, they would probably react as differently as the three items in my experiment, namely, the egg and potato in the first two experiments and the coffee in the third.

Things are constantly changing around us, be it in business or life. What is critically important is how we react to these changes and what we make of them. It is all about learning, adapting and converting our problems and challenges into success. Our reaction or response has the power to turn a potentially negative situation into a positive one.

In the experiment mentioned above, all three items had to be boiled in water. I had to boil the egg for eight minutes, the potato for ten minutes and the coffee beans till I could smell the magical aroma of coffee. Boiling the item for a little too long or too little would not give the desired results. In business, you have to be constantly conscious about what your specimen needs—whether you are dealing with eggs, potatoes or coffee beans—in the form of everyday situations. You must have all three abilities, namely, the ability to boil an egg or potato and the skill to make perfect coffee using roasted coffee beans.

In over three decades I have observed that many businessmen are not able to clearly identify and define their role in their sector. Due to lack of clarity, they often face unnecessary stress and strain. In the very early stages of my business I identified the three types of businessmen. I have played all these roles in my various businesses, and these definitions have aided me in the process. I suggest that you understand your own three roles just as clearly. You may even have to be a combination of all three of these types to fulfil the needs of your business.

1. The Helicopter Businessman, who, on starting a new business, has to be present the entire day. Such a businessman cannot afford to leave his station and establishment; he has to oversee almost everything in the same way that a helicopter hovers in the air. Such a businessman has to be a helicopter—watching from afar, but fully present while the business is in its initial stages.
2. The Aeroplane Businessman, who after having established his business and ensured it's smooth running, may not need to be present to attend to the various activities. Such a businessman can afford to keep an eye on his business from a distance. This businessman has provided his establishment with a runway, and the business has already taken off. It can now run in autopilot mode.
3. The Fighter Jet Businessman, who is required to rush in and save the day during an emergency. As a fighter jet businessman, he must rush to the business in case of any need. After having solved the problem, he can then return to his original place or position.

Understanding the importance, relevance and use of each of the three roles has greatly helped me in all my businesses. Become a combination of all three and perform your role as per the needs of your business.

A common mistake that many businessmen commit is that they are not able to identify themselves or their roles properly in their business. Let me explain this by taking up an illustration. It is necessary to identify yourself at the outset. For example, when you first start your business, you give all your time and attention to it. You are then a helicopter businessman. You draft your own correspondences and meet all your clients. You also operate from your PC (personal computer). You manage the procurement of raw materials and devote time to quality. Since you know the banking requirements of your business well, you don't delegate it to anyone else. You also have time to innovate on the product and its packaging. You manage the quality assurance. You spend time attending to marketing your products or services. You also manage payment collections from clients. Once the other tasks are efficiently done, you formulate expansion plans.

But once your business has picked up, you build a team of employees and outsource certain jobs and activities. Your business has now taken off from the runway you have provided. You can no longer attend regular affairs; this will be done by other team members now. You have assigned duties and have also delegated responsibilities. You have defined the powers, financial and otherwise, that each functionary in your business enjoys. As an aeroplane businessman, you can now stay away and still manage your business well.

Finally, as a fighter jet businessman, you may be called in whenever there is a crisis of any sort or during the annual closing of accounts, quarterly or annual stocktaking, inspections by government agencies and the statutory audits, etc.

Clearly identifying your role in your business, particular to your situation, will help you run it smoothly and efficiently. These three differing and complementary roles become even more important when you have multiple businesses to run! Happy flying!

AGILITY IS CAPABILITY

13

KALYUG KI SANJIVANI

Hindu scriptures will tell you of Lord Hanuman, the most ardent devotee of Rama. It is believed that all the monkeys on this earth are the descendants of 'Lord Hanuman'.

Lord Hanuman is the epitome of devotion (bhakti) and valour. He is worshipped as the lord of wisdom, knowledge, strength, devotion, courage and self-discipline.

In the holy book Sri Ramcharitmanas, Lord Rama's younger brother, Lakshmana, faints during a battle with Ravana's son, Meghnad. Sushen, a renowned vaidya or medical practitioner from Lanka, is brought to the battlefield by Hanuman. Sushen examines Lakshmana and says that his life can only be saved through the use of a rare herb, the sanjivani booti. There are other conditions: the rare plant must be plucked from the peak of the Himalayan range and brought to him before daybreak. Only Hanuman possessed the strength to traverse such a long distance in such a short period of time. Sushen explained how Hanuman was to recognize the particular herb from amongst many other plants on the mountain range.

Hanuman overcame many hurdles on his way to the Himalayas. But upon reaching the mountain range, he found that all the herbs and plants looked similar; he was unable to identify the right one, the sanjivani booti. Therefore, he uprooted and picked up the entire mountain—Dronagiri—and carried it on the palm of his hand back to the battlefield.

He reached the field before sunset. Sushen prepared the medicine and administered it to Lakshmana, and the dying Lakshmana regained consciousness in no time. But Hanuman was only able to rush to the Himalayas, lift and bring the entire mountain, and fly back in time because he too is a god.

Businesses have their own vaidyas in the form of consultants. Consultants for income tax, goods and services tax (GST), export and imports, investments, civil and criminal issues, corporate affairs, and so on, each of them a specialist in their own field. However, even if you do your best you cannot possess the qualities and attributes that Hanuman did to save your business. Instead, you need to learn to identify and administer the applicable sanjivani bootis for your business. That is to say, you must acquire a working knowledge of the various rules, regulations and applicable laws, as far as your business is concerned. Acquiring this knowledge should be an ongoing process, with its own timely updates.

I provide a few examples of necessary bases you should cover in the course of your business.

To begin, it is essential for any business to maintain an account book to control its operations. Be well versed with basic knowledge of accounting and regulations, even if you have employed professionals such as chartered accountants or cost accountants to assist you.

Apart from the rules pertaining to personal taxation and income tax, knowledge of corporate taxation, various rebates available, refund procedures, penalties and other similar provisions will aid you greatly.

Similarly, while customs duty may not be applicable to all businesses, knowledge of excise laws is essential for all businesses engaged in manufacturing goods. Recognize what your business needs are and plan accordingly.

The introduction of GST has greatly simplified the law relating to sales tax, but as your turnover increases, the burden of compliance also goes up. Additionally, there are strict timelines to fill various returns pertaining to GST. You must know the nitty-gritty of these rules so no violations occur due to ignorance. Knowledge of social security schemes available to Indian employees, namely, the employee state insurance and provident fund, will give you insights on the eligibility of your establishment or factory under the different labour laws and rules and the mandatory contribution of employers in each case. Be updated on the prevailing employment and labour laws to handle work situations with confidence, ensure prompt decision-making and provide for occupational health and safety.

You must also be conversant with the provisions with respect to capital raising, business loans, overdraft facilities, cash credit limits, etc. Your lack of knowledge will only hurt you. Many private financiers are on the prowl.

Registration of companies and the filing of various statutory returns are complex matters, but gradually acquiring a working knowledge to manoeuvre is absolutely essential for any modern businessman. The rules pertaining to weights and measures are applicable to nearly every business organization today and some foundation knowledge of this aspect is necessary. Every businessman must have basic knowledge about

ADAPT TO DIFFERENT FREQUENCIES

the applicability of copyright rules, trademark rules and regulations, patents, violations and penalties prescribed by the law. The relevance of digital marketing must be understood to extend your reach to a larger audience. Online marketing is different from offline marketing and so it is imperative to understand and learn how to deal with the online platform first.

Finally, every year the Union budget presented by the Union finance minister will bring its own surprises. You must always be alert to developments in this regard.

Though consultants may be readily available to you, you will only be able to capitalize on their services when you are equipped with the basic knowledge of the field. Need-based guidance will propel and help you expand your business. This may be a tedious and time-consuming process, but it is the need of the hour.

I see the various solutions and knowledge mentioned above as if they are the 'sanjivani bootis' for my business and the various professionals and consultants as the modern-day 'vaidyas'. What really matters for any business is taking need-based guidance from various consultants. You must have the will to acquire the skills required for identifying each sanjivani booti and go forth!

14

YOUR FIRST DRIVER

In the summer of 2019, I was fortunate enough to visit the Indian School of Business (ISB) in Hyderabad. The campus was established in 2001 at a beautiful site spread across 260 acres.

I visited the campus with an agenda. I was to address their student cell on the theme of building an inclusive society. Since I am constantly in a wheelchair, I understand the different barriers that one faces in the physical environment. I was asked to sensitize the selected audience through various interactions and multiple awareness sessions. I also was to meet and advise two student groups working on start-ups, largely based on my entrepreneurial experience in the education sector.

However, I also wanted to voluntarily take a tour of the ISB campus to ascertain their disability accessibility and preparedness. Admittedly, such accessibility audits interest me and I am generally available for them. I was happy to find that the ISB campus was almost 80 per cent accessible for wheelchair users. The team was humble and promised to work on some suggestions I made.

Later during the visit, I was keen to learn from ISB how we should run our Rishihood University. To understand this, I had to meet the faculty and make sense of how ISB works, especially with respect to humanitarian aspects. I wanted to know about their distinct ideology and their incubation centre. I spent two long days within the campus, socializing and learning from the students, faculty members and human resource (HR) department. The free and frank discussion and the pleasant environment made me want to remain there. Perhaps I had fallen in love with their architecture and atmosphere.

The opportunity to meet with students working on two different start-ups is of particular relevance here.

The students shared the details of their project. Their idea, concept, market study, beta version, day-to-day understanding, progress and further plan of action were well charted out. As my meeting came to a close, I rose to address them.

'Well, I am indeed impressed with your project and the clarity you have shown here. Now, can each one of you please tell me as to what is that one thing that will really drive your business to its success? What is that single essential prerequisite for achieving success in any business?'

One student replied, 'Appropriate fundraising!'

Another student answered, 'The right marketing strategies.'

A third student answered with conviction, 'The right customers, correct sales pitch and our knowledge of our customers will aid us.'

The fourth student added, 'I believe pricing is that one thing that will ensure our success in our start-up world.'

The second group of students answered in much the same way and were also close to the answers given by group one.

I was impressed that even before the students met me, they had studied my profile. These two start-ups were related to Edutech and they had expected that since I came from the education segment, I would be able to add value.

Based on my personal knowledge and experience, I gave them my advice with particular reference to the factors mentioned by each one of them. I wished them good luck and took their leave. Much later, on the way to the airport, I felt a little disappointed that none of these bright students had mentioned the right answer: Passion. Passion is a prerequisite for success in their business venture, particularly when it comes to a start-up.

What is passion? It is an admixture containing excitement in whatever you do, a belief in your products and services, the ambition of becoming successful and concentration in your action. Your passion should reflect the combination of far-sightedness, love and willpower. If any of these elements are missing, try to fill the gaps.

When you are passionate about something, you rise even above the most complex challenges related to time, future uncertainties, loss of control and varied outcomes. You need to have immense faith in your passion to do anything. Your passion gives you limitless energy and a vision for the future.

Different businesses, based on their nature and type, demand different things from you. If you are passionate about your business then please try to fulfil its demands. Only you can fulfil the demands of your business. There is none other to do so.

If your business requires travelling then transform your travel needs into your passion. Don't accept it as a requirement of the business or consider it as a burden. Instead, please start to enjoy it. Similarly, if your business requires late nights working at the office then prepare yourself accordingly. Tune your sleep cycle accordingly. After some time, working in night shift should become your passion.

Similarly, if networking, knowledge upgradation and extra qualifications are necessities in your business then make these necessities your passion. This is possible with a little effort and a little conviction, followed by an effort made on a regular basis. Passion can become the backbone of your business.

Here I am giving you a simple mantra that is tried and tested. I believe that since it works well with me, it will work well for you too. For example, you will have to tell yourself, 'I am passionate about travelling. I am looking to challenge myself and learn the art of enjoyment during my travel. I will gift myself something during this, like a special dish while visiting different people throughout the day during my travel.'

Affirming yourself in this manner will regularly lead to developing passion in that task. If you describe your need to your inner self, gradually it becomes your passion.

I know from personal experience that beliefs play a very important role in shaping your success and your destiny. I believe that for any business to flourish, it is only passion that drives you—it is your first driver. You must be in love with your business venture. Your affection and care will definitely help you nourish your business well. To put it simply, have passion for your business and if you don't, develop it!

FERVOUR NOURISHES BUSINESSES

15

AACHAR KI BARNI

I recall a particular week during winter in Delhi many years ago. The last three days had been cloudy and windy, without any sunshine. The chill in the air and the biting wind had left people nearly frozen and in low spirits. People longed for a bright and sunny day to bring some respite.

On the fourth day, the sun shone. It rose bright in all its glory as if smiling gleefully at our plight. Pawan's terrace benefited; it gleamed. The children had been enjoying their winter break from school but the last few days had been spent indoors, shivering in the cold. Pleased at the prospect of a long sunny day, they left their homes with their cricket gear and headed straight for the neighbourhood park.

Pawan's grandfather, a seventy-five-year-old man had weak knees; the pain was chronic. With the sun shining bright, he too breathed a sigh of relief. He took out a bottle of massage oil and headed for the terrace. After a long moment spent basking in the sun, he finally took some oil and began to massage his legs and knees. He sat content in the soothing sun on the roof of his ancestral house.

Pawan's mother was also on the terrace. The clothes that she had washed in the last three days had not yet dried. She picked them up, even the blankets, and carried them to place them in the sun.

Pawan's affectionate grandmother carefully picked up her ceramic jar brimming with fresh pickle. It needed to be placed in the light of the sun before she could allow her family members to relish it. She was quick to grab some peanuts on her way; she would sit on the terrace, peel them and enjoy the sunshine. Once on the terrace, she is very particular about not leaving her ceramic jar of pickles unattended even for a minute, lest some birds cause damage to her delicacies.

Pawan's father had been working on a solar energy project. He had been waiting eagerly for the sun to shine. He quickly picked up his apparatus and equipment for the experiment and headed the roof. He settled in his favourite corner where he thought the sun's rays would shine the brightest till late in the evening.

You will notice that the blazing sun shone equally brightly for everyone in Pawan's household. The sun's rays had the same heat and light for each family member on that terrace; each family member had an equal opportunity to benefit from it. But everyone individually chose to use the sun's energy in his or her own way. Each family member simply wanted to utilize this opportunity in line with the priorities that they had already set.

When the sun shines, it throws open innumerable possibilities before each one of us. The sun is just one single entity; the beneficiaries are many, each of them with multiple priorities and options in front of them. In business, the situation is similar. Every businessman gets different opportunities in different situations. As a businessman, you need to tap into and productively use the energies that different opportunities provide to build a successful business.

The way shade and sunshine are both part of our life, change and opportunities are also part of our business scenarios. Opportunities are sometimes not clearly visible, not in the way sunshine is. Sometimes we are unable to recognize these opportunities, or we recognize them too late. You need to identify your business opportunities.

Look at these general opportunities, for example. The market is now ready for technology in the process of imparting education. The concept is quickly gaining acceptance and growth in Tier II and Tier III cities of India, regions that are considered markets with great potential.

With the advent of digitization, you can now build smart businesses. State-of-the-art technologies have made it possible to convert information into binary code; information technology (IT) is the new road to improving customer relationships, analysing trends. The government is unlocking tremendous potential by promoting aspiring districts in India, hoping to transform them and create business opportunities. Free trade zones (FTZ) and SEZs also provide many benefits to businesses in terms of incentives, exemptions, tax deductions, borrowing ease and more.

FDI has increased in India leading to ease of doing business for start-ups, encouraging innovation and implementation. Start-ups enjoy benefits such as tax holidays, R&D facilities, cost reduction, tax savings, simplified/simple policies and procedures and more. Additionally, there are rises in both service-oriented industries and manufacturing industries.

In the same way that Pawan's grandfather and grandmother are always prepared to harness the energies of the blazing sun's rays, we as businessmen must also be always ready to grab opportunities for our business to flourish. With a population of nearly 1.38 billion, India

SEIZE THE MOMENT

is second only to China in terms of demographic size. We have the potential of becoming the central node of global business opportunities across various sectors. The changing trends in consumer behaviour and the constant increase in pocket size have led to rapid urbanization. India will be the land of opportunities. Metropolitan cities are expected to reach stagnation in business, especially when compared to Tier II and Tier III cities which are likely to pull investors. Other developed countries are also looking towards developing economies to expand their portfolio. This again triggers the possibilities in our country. Now, it depends on us. Can we see the bright future ahead? We need to synchronize our future possibilities with our businesses and plan its development in different phases.

The sun shines on everyone equally; the possibilities are unlimited and you only need to recognize and grab them. Some call it luck. But I prefer to say that luck favours the prepared.

16

A COIN HAS MANY SIDES

Every coin has two sides, they say—not one but two options. However, I believe that every coin has not only two but many sides to it. More often than not, we have multiple options to choose from.

I was watching a concert in 1991 on YouTube with my wife. This concert was by the world-renowned musician Zubin Mehta. He wore a garland of fresh roses around his neck and with every vigorous move, a few rose petals would fall to the ground. While watching, I joked with my wife that if this continued, Zubin would soon only have only a thread around his neck.

My wife, an intelligent woman, said, 'Why would you be staring at the thread? Shouldn't you be gladdened by the bed of lovely rose petals on the floor?'

'Whenever you lose something, you also get something in return, isn't it?' she added. Her response left me speechless. It made me think about one of my favourite sayings, which has become part of my belief system: there is nothing like failure; what people often call failure is only a stepping stone to success. *When you lose something, you gain something else in return.*

Whether you take your so-called failures as utter disasters or simply as stepping stones to success depends entirely upon your attitude. This attitude applies equally to your personal as well as your working life. I dedicate this story to entrepreneurs who have had a failed start-up but have not given up and have, instead, moved on to start another start-up with renewed vigour and zeal. For the sake of simplicity and keeping your reading and comprehension smooth, in this write-up I shall refer to such stepping stones as failures only.

When we talk about failed start-ups, which are aplenty in any country, we cannot omit to talk about the failed start-ups in Israel.

Israel is known to have the highest number of start-ups among all the countries of the world. However, Israel is also home to the highest number of failed start-ups.

Israel is a world leader in autonomous driving, cybersecurity, enterprise software, clean technology and digital health, in addition to many other fields. It is home to thousands of start-ups, hundreds of angel investors, dozens of accelerators and various other useful resources. The technology ecosystem in Israel continues to grow and has produced enormous success. The result is that today, Israel is known as a start-up nation. In Israel, whenever a start-up fails, the entrepreneur has to follow a certain tradition. He has to, perforce, throw a party to celebrate the occasion.

This ensures that the individual keeps up his spirits and he continues to enjoy the same pride and status he earlier held. This is enough to keep him motivated to start afresh. This is the attitude necessary. A bad incident or a situation ignites two subconscious thoughts: one leads to negativity and the other leads to positivity. In general, unconsciously, negative thoughts overpower our minds and block the free flow of other thoughts. At times, repeated events convince us that there is no other option. This is when we don't see the other side of the same situation which may have more potential or maybe the remedial option. Just sit, have a cup of coffee, talk to your buddy or mentor and brainstorm. You can do fishbone analysis on a piece of paper to explore several sides of the same coin. Amazon, the American multinational technology e-commerce company, has finally started diversifying by opening physical retail stores by the name of Amazon Go. Similarly, Netflix, a DVD (digital versatile disc) rental company, has changed the way we spend our free time. Netflix.shop is a new American e-commerce site dedicated to selling exclusive but limited editions of curated material and collectible products tied to its shows and brands. Hence, a business can have many sides. Beauty lies in the eyes of the beholder. Similarly, options lie in the eyes of the observer.

Before you decide to begin your own start-up, you must have your product validated. To begin, conduct appropriate market study/market research, checking for the availability of a market for your end product. Similarly, look to professionals who are already established in your field and take the necessary approvals from venture capitalists/investors and requisite feedback from prospective competitors.

Now, you must both hope for the best *and* be prepared for the worst. Right from the planning stage to actual implementation, you must be prepared and equipped to handle desirable *and* undesirable situations. In addition to considering business-as-usual scenarios, you must already have prepared to change lanes in other scenarios.

Remember, every failure teaches you what mistakes you must not make the next time.

This is not a small or unimportant lesson. When questioned on his repeated 'failures' while trying to invent the electric bulb, Albert Einstein said that each time his experiment did not yield the desired results, he considered himself successful in as much as he now knew 'what he should not do the next time'. He felt that this was important for him if he wished to be successful in his experiment. Yes, it's a question of having the right attitude.

Any failure tells you that you may have erred in determining the right finances, the right customers, the right market, the right time, the right marketing strategy, and so on. Now all you have to do is your homework and identify what is just right for your start-up business venture. What is right today remains right for your business for all time that is yet to come.

When you look back at the resources, processes, pitch, marketing campaigns, etc., you will realize that you had the option to choose and pick the most effective tools. You may have made mistakes. Introspection will ensure that you do not err when you start your next venture.

The reasons for failure are never the same for different businesses or businessmen. To understand better and identify the root causes, it is important to ponder over these particular reasons. Every time you review your own condition, many new reasons for not being successful will unfold. Your early discovery of the various reasons contributing to your failures/mistakes in business will help you in identifying ways for their quick elimination.

Always flip your coin and look for more results.

YOUR
PERCEPTION
OF YOURSELF
BECOMES
YOUR REALITY

17

WHO SETS YOUR BUSINESS GOALS?

Once, a rider atop a horse was galloping away to glory. In his haste, he almost ran over a fellow man.

Shocked, the stumbling man yelled at the top of his voice, 'Where do you think you are going?'

The rider replied indifferently. 'Don't ask me. Ask my horse!'

Taking a clue from this short anecdote, we sometimes find ourselves in the rider's position, being dragged against our will.

We give away control of our lives and our businesses to other people who run them based on their whims and fancies. We lose control of our own affairs or our business affairs. In such a scenario, we stop using our wisdom and judgement and simply follow directions. And the strange part is that we often don't even realize that our lives or businesses are being controlled by someone else!

If this is true in your case, wherein you are no longer setting your own business goals and someone is doing it for you, then are you really running the business? Or is the business running you? Of course, you are likely to cause an accident. You may even face a major loss.

Isn't it time you took charge of your own business?

In business, if you do not clearly outline your goals, you should not expect to reach your destination. Goals should be accurate, articulated, well thought out and directly proportionate to your purpose and your target. Do not allow anybody else to decide these goals on your behalf. Chances are that he or she may not be acquainted with *your* vision.

Before I proceed any further, I would like you to look at the significance of setting business goals. This is as important as setting your destination before you embark upon your journey. At times, it so happens that you decide to set up a business and the journey starts. Meanwhile, when certain unwanted changes occur within the external or internal ecosystem, we start considering quitting or changing our business goals altogether. It is important to define business goals but they must be integrated/aligned with the departmental goals and the individual's goal.

Think about it. Are your business goals further divided into departmental goals and individual goals? Are key performance indicators (KPIs) set up properly? Do you have R&D teams to innovate and upgrade the existing systems? All these elements will enrich your goals. Goals lead to revenue generation, especially if your goals are well articulated considering all these aspects.

As an entrepreneur, you should be the only one setting these goals and identifying these destinations. The goals may differ from situation to situation. Some goals are short term while others extend into the long run; some must be achieved in their entirety, while others may be partially fulfilled; some goals are particular while others are held in common.

There are benefits to setting these goals. When your focus areas are well defined, your employees are motivated and aware of their priorities and the direction of the company. Knowing and communicating your business goals helps promote teamwork; group incentives motivate team members to work as a team to earn rewards. Setting a goal helps boost the morale of your investors and employees, increases productivity and in turn, increases profitability. It also helps measure success and achievements during every quarter and correct the course of action, wherever required.

You can set different types of goals for your business.

For example, you can try to reduce your fixed and variable expenses, commit to better fund management and utilization, formulate contemporary recruitment, selection, training and responsibility indicators, or take initiatives to improve systems of inflow and outflow.

You can look for technical collaborations and expansions. It is good to open units at other locations and to increase your overseas trade and presence.

You can focus on building your brand and improving your online footprint.

Additionally, you can attempt to increase your sales and turnover for better profitability, while working on adding newer products to your existing line. In this regard, quality assurance and customer services should be prioritized.

The list of goals may be endless but you must ensure that your short-term goals are aligned with your long-term goals. Remember to measure your ability to meet each goal on a periodic basis, modifying or expanding on the goal when necessary.

Once you have set these goals for your business, you should try to make each goal smarter. A smart goal is measurable, specific, achievable,

YOUR START, YOUR STORY

relevant to your business and is time based. For instance, instead of a goal that abstractly attempts to increase market share, you should set a more specific goal. *I will increase my overall market share by at least 2 per cent before the end of the year!* This is a smart goal.

Do not let anyone else set your business goals for you. Don't let the flow of the business dictate your path. Set your own smart business goals in line with your own value systems and business ethics. Let your business run at a pace that you have decided upon.

18

NEVER GIVE UP

At dawn each day, a mystic went down to the river to wash himself. After his bath, he would stand knee-deep in the river and pray to the sun god. He faced the east, brought his palms together, held water from the river, raised them above his head and then he reverentially offered this water to the sun god. This was his daily ritual.

One day, as the mystic cupped his palms to raise the water to the god, he saw a deadly scorpion. Within a split second, the scorpion had stung him. Reflexively, he shouted and dropped the holy water and the scorpion back into the river.

His ritual had been interrupted. He bent and tried to continue once again, cupping his hands to hold the riverine water. But the scorpion raised its tail once again and mystic was stung.

The mystic did not give up. He repeated this a few times, and was stung every time he tried.

A young disciple sat quietly by the side of the river and watched his teacher fail. He said nothing.

After many such thwarted attempts, the mystic finally completed his ritual. When the mystic emerged tired from the river, the disciple could not hold himself back.

'O my Guru,' he began to ask, 'when the scorpion stung you, why didn't you immediately throw him out on to the bank of the river? Why didn't you move a few feet away? Why didn't you skip the offering today? Why didn't you do any of these things?'

The mystic politely replied, 'My dear child, when the poisonous and deadly scorpion, merely an insect, was doing his assigned job with such diligence, dedication and passion, how could it have been appropriate for me, a mere mystic, to change my course?'

The young disciple was chastened and hung his head.

If you too want to be successful in business, you must be like the mystic.

The mystic had a never-give-up attitude. Businessmen should take lessons from the attitude of mystics like these and understand where they must give up and where they must stay strong in their business journey. If you talk about me, I am already in the 'Never Give Up' club. I follow twenty rules to succeed according to this attitude, on both the personal and the professional front. Every business is different and have different challenges but these rules hold true for the most part in all scenarios.

1. Never give up on goodness and do try to make it one of the core values of your business. When you are your best version, you encourage a culture of goodness. This drives us towards better business results. Your business will exceed the client's

expectations when goodness is apparent in your products and services.

2. Never give up on offering true value to your customers. You may be tempted to cut corners to increase your profits in the initial phase of your business but in the long run, the relationship between perceived value and true value will lead to repeat business deals.
3. Don't give up on your 'Aha!' moments. Work hard to create these moments or savour them when they come around, making strategic use of it. Induce 'Aha!' moments in business by manifesting them and make better decisions. There is a direct relationship between your success and your persistence in following through these moments.
4. Don't ignore the need to prioritize your tasks. Prioritizing increases the rate of success in a business and improves the quality of work. Planning your day-to-day work allows you to focus on high-value tasks and take control of your workload. The best method to follow while prioritizing is the well-known 80–20 rule.
5. Never give up on unlearning and relearning as this process will keep you relevant in your industry. Expand your mind by gaining new knowledge; see carefully and think carefully. You are always learning.
6. Don't give up on your winning attitude as it is the pathway to business success. Your attitude makes you better, optimistic, proactive and it allows you to think big. Your attitude will keep your subconscious mind powerful and it will directly impact your ability to keep everything in business intact and competitive.

7. Don't give up on trying new modes of advertisement in business. If compelled to give up, spend time exploring the latest trends. There has been a global shift in the mindset of the customer and the agility in their behaviour; this has given rise to many new ways of getting your product connected with your target customers. Your business is no longer restricted to specific demographics. Moreover, contemporary trends in advertisement increase the reach of your brand and product.
8. Don't let your creativity lose its shine. Fuel it with new and innovative ways regularly to be distinctive in the business. You can be creative in your pitch, product, service, support, interaction, relationship building, gestures, and so on. You can make your style statement with creativity and communicate your business offerings.
9. Don't give up on digitalization! It is now compulsory in the twenty-first century. Your business needs an online presence on social media handles like Facebook, LinkedIn, YouTube, Twitter and others. Keep faith in the use of technology and don't hesitate to try the new and latest tools on the block. Many applications are user friendly and enable you to manage your personal and professional goals more efficiently. Make sure that your financial budget includes a macro budget where you allocate funds to spend on digitization, which caters not only to the marketing of your product but also enhances the purpose of your organization.
10. Don't stop surprising your family and extended family members, including your business partners, employees and clients. Everyone must feel good—even at work!
11. Never give up on accepting and sharing feedback. Honest

feedback can be a life changer. It can help your business and its people go a long way towards improvement of the self, the product or the services. Honest feedback can also assist your organization in fine-tuning at various stages, right from planning to the execution of various aspects. Treat feedback like a mirror in which you can view your company. But remember, feedback must be taken with care.

12. Never give up on R&D in business and keep it going. No matter how busy you are, you deserve to explore new perspectives. You may not feel interested in the beginning, but keep exploring this aspect from different angles until you find something you can feast on and digest well. So read, research, analyse, upgrade and innovate to add the X-factor to your business.
13. Don't give up on celebrations in the business. Being an Indian, you ought to celebrate days of national importance, such as Independence Day and feel pride in one's own country. Similarly, celebratory occasions like the brand's anniversary should be rung in with the stakeholders to lend a sense of pride in the organization. Celebrations relax the mind, bring joy, give you a reason to treasure milestones and accomplishments, bringing new life to your working style and much more. Keep celebrating.
14. Never give up on expressing yourself as a visionary businessman. Let your imagination and thoughts be understood by those working with you. Sometimes, a few words and a few details about the vision, projects and end goals can aid in the process of brainstorming with the people around you.
15. Don't give up on appreciating others. A pat on the back is desired by all who make an effort, whether they are good or

simply competent. Devise new ways of appreciating your team. A few words of appreciation can do wonders and lifts souls, improving productivity and efficiency at work.

16. Never give up on quality assurance. Build a culture in the organization towards keeping an eye on the deviations in the implementation of SOPs which can raise issues regarding non-conformity. Due to globalization, business, product line expansion, quality assurance has become critical. It is like having an 'Inspector' at your organization. Remember that sometimes our critics can play an important role in improving existing practices and methodologies.
17. Don't forget to be grateful for the life you have. Take out time to thank the people around you. Feel gratitude for the business and its sustainability with the help of people who serve directly or indirectly.
18. Don't give up on your humanity. As a businessman, you can make a socio-economic impact in society. A business not only sustains itself but also countless others engaged alongside it—in terms of employment or service providers. As a businessman, you can make a radical difference in society by implementing projects for the less privileged or undertaking other philanthropic ventures.
19. Never give up revising. Your processes need revisions regularly, as do your products, your costings, your brand and other areas. Allot yourself time to think on what can be revised in your business environment.
20. Never give up on your personal life. It is good to immerse oneself in the business, but do strive to create a work-life balance. Spend quality time with your family on weekends

FIGHT HARD TO STAY IN THE GAME

or after work hours. This will make you happy, energetic and satisfied. After all, life is lived only once.

Much like these twenty rules, there may be other aspects, procedures and ways that should be taken care of. Keep holding on to your never-give-up attitude!

19

CALORIE CONSCIOUS

Some people are extremely conscious of their health requirements. Whether their diet or their exercise regime, they follow a strict plan. Look to Mr Tijay Gupta, a thirty-five-year-old businessman. He weighs 60 kg and is 5 feet and 5 inches tall. He wakes at 6.30 a.m. in summers and between 7.15 a.m. and 7.30 a.m. in winters.

He follows a strict routine: he has a cup of black coffee, three almonds and 50 gm of walnuts (occasionally replacing the coffee with a cup of green tea). He does yoga for an hour, followed by a brisk walk for half an hour. His breakfast always includes a cup of hot milk or fresh juice, two eggs and toasted bread with jam. For lunch, he has a bowl of poha, two rotis, one cup of dal and one bowl of rice—preferably brown rice. In the evening, he snacks on two biscuits with a cup of tea/coffee and a small bowl of fruit chaat or a bowl of sprouts. His dinner is equally simple. A green salad or some steamed vegetables are good enough. Mr Gupta consumes more than two litres of water every day to detox his body. Furthermore, he enjoys munching on roasted black gram all through the day.

This amounts to a calorie intake of between 1,500 and 1,800. He burns between 1,500 and 1,800 every day. Mr Gupta allows himself four cheat days every month, though he prefers not to use them all the time. However, following this routine does not mean that he will never fall sick, but it does increase his immunity and fitness.

You too need a well-balanced, well-planned and effective budget in order to run a successful business, whether small or not. It is a myth that small businesses need not have a budget. On the contrary, the need for a budget in small- and medium-sized businesses is higher.

Before you start preparing your business budget, you will have to peep into the future of your business. Have a futuristic approach and contemplate where you can take your business in the near and not-so-near future. A business budget can be divided into three parts: short-term budget, medium-term budget and long-term budget. These are self-explanatory, but note that the long-term budget will provide you with a road map for the future. Within this budget, the amounts that you allocate to each head will be directly proportional to the emphasis that you intend to place on that segment at that particular point in time. It will help you stay on track as far as your business is concerned.

Your business budget will have to be further divided into many accounting heads, each of which will be important. The budget should ideally be divided into a monthly budget, a quarterly budget and an annual budget. While budgeting, you may have to start from the annual budget and then work your way backwards. I will point to a few critical accounting heads below.

For a continuous increase in sales and growth of your business, it is important that you generate new enquiries. If your business is relatively new, you may have to have a higher budget for marketing, advertising and sales promotion. You will also have to explore new avenues such as digital marketing and zero or low-cost advertising. This is one of the first heads in your budget.

As soon as you start generating profits, you must set aside sufficient funds for meeting future contingencies. This is the second important head. These reserves strengthen the financial position of your business. Further, in a challenging or difficult business environment, such reserves become your internal source of financing. They also help avoid debts or the need to raise funds at exorbitant rates of interest for meeting sudden business obligations. If your business activities involve high risk, then such reserves should be at a higher level.

Remember to include a budget head for innovation, R&D of new products/services. They can provide you with some USPs—not only for increasing your sales and profits but also in dealing with environmental issues and incubation period challenges. Your business segment will determine how much you ought to budget under this head. For instance, if you are in the IT business, this amount will be relatively higher.

No business can thrive or even survive by taking new loans to meet its needs without a system to service the loans already taken. You must include this in your budget to make timely repayment of all loans, big and small, along with the interest due thereon. This will also help you improve your credit rating and build goodwill.

Moreover, account for the fact that all equipment and machinery that you use in your business will need replacement/repairs. It may be due to normal wear and tear, sudden breakdown or damage to plant and machinery, technological advancement, need for automation, reduction in manpower or any other factor. Having an adequate budget to meet this capital expenditure is absolutely necessary.

Entrepreneurs must also be particular with their budgets. Their expenses are likely to rise with every passing year. They must budget for salaries and wages, provident fund contributions, employees' medical expense/reimbursements/bonuses, power and electricity, government taxes, legal expenses, other professional fees, office utilities and the like. Inflation has an impact on your business and annual hikes can neither be ignored nor avoided. Suitable budgeting for meeting such incremental expenses is of utmost importance.

Wise businessmen also say that you must have a contingency fund or reserve to meet your personal expenses for at least six months. These expenses are different from your normal business expenses. Having a budget to provide for this reserve or contingency fund will help you sail through difficult times.

Business budgeting is a detailed exercise. It can only be done after taking into account the financials for the previous year, the current year (actual and anticipated) and the best estimates for the following year. Though many accounting heads may be common for a lot of businesses, specific items must be taken into consideration depending upon the nature of your business. For any business budget to be realistic, you must have a clear idea about the various items of income and expenditure concerning your business. Make sure to involve all the concerned members of your business team in the budgeting exercise as well. It will help you make it better. Business budgeting must be in tune with the organizational goals. You must follow the practice of external forecasting of the business environment and make it part of your SOPs as it helps in long-term organizational development. Make adequate provisions for a contingency budget to be utilized if such a need arises. With technological advancement and global competitiveness, our budgeting must also be dynamic in nature.

Establish your calorie-conscious business to have better immunity

INVEST WISELY, REAP INDEFINITELY

and chances at success through budgeting. To set up such a business that has an ideal immunity, you need to first recognize the importance of budgeting in business. Learn to prepare a dynamic budget and make it a habit to prepare your business budget regularly. Most importantly, remember that the budget must be need-appropriate. Your sound health as an entrepreneur and a well-planned business depends on it.

20

THE METRO SITUATION

You go to the metro station to catch a train. But when you are on the platform, the train arrives on time and you are not able to board for one reason or another. Now, what do you do? Do you go back home? Or do you wait for the next train and if necessary, the one after that as well?

Safin Hasan, the youngest Indian Police Service (IPS) officer, was born in a typical lower-middle-class family in Gujarat. He was twenty-two years old at the time of his selection into the prestigious service.

Safin's parents worked in a diamond polishing unit to feed the family and to educate their son. Safin's father had even worked as an electrician, doing small jobs in the village households, while his mother cooked food for a few families in the neighbourhood.

Safin studied in a government school where the main medium of conversation between the students was Gujarati; little emphasis was paid to teaching the English language. By the time he reached high school, he found that while his classmates from affluent families conversed in English, he was a misfit. He could not speak English at all.

Safin was in his eleventh year of school when he realized that he could either go home and cry his heart out or he could start learning the language from scratch. He chose the second option.

In 2017, while Safin was on his way to appear for the written examination to join the civil services, the UPSC (union public service commission), he met with an accident. The ligament of his knee was torn and he sustained injuries on his head and his left hand. But when he looked at his right hand, he realized that despite his severe injuries, he could perhaps manage to write with his right hand. In that moment of crisis, he made a really bold decision. Instead of going to a hospital for first aid to be administered, he decided to appear for his written examination in his injured state.

His injuries were so severe that immediately after the written examination ended, he had to be admitted to a hospital for surgeries.

Months later, the results arrived and Safin had gotten through the first hurdle. His interview had been scheduled for March 2018. He had to prepare. However, more trials awaited him. A month before the interview, he had to be admitted to the hospital due to a urinary tract infection and issues with his white blood cells. He was discharged a few days before the interview. He left for Delhi to prepare for the interview with the help of expert coaches at a coaching institute. But within two days, he fell sick and had to fly back to Gujarat to be hospitalized. He was finally discharged just three days before the interview. Despite his medical conditions and intermittent preparation, Safin appeared and spoke at length during his interview.

He was the second-highest scorer when the results of the interview were announced. Safin later joined the IPS in 2019 as Assistant Superintendent of Police at Jamnagar in Gujarat.

Even the master blaster Sachin Tendulkar had fared badly during the most important match of his career. The One Day International (ODI) cricket match where he could not score even a single run. However, he stayed on the team and went on to hit numerous centuries, creating history since then.

In life and business, many occasions will challenge you. At these junctures, you can simply give up, go home and cry. Or, you can stay back, fight the odds and often, come out a winner. The choice is always yours! I like to refer to the situation above as 'The Metro Situation'. If you have lived and grown up in a big city with its own metro line, then it is likely that you will be able to effortlessly board the first metro train that comes your way.

On the contrary, if you hailed from a small town then boarding an overcrowded train may have been tougher for you in a big city. What if you are carrying a heavy briefcase and you decide to let the first overcrowded metro go? What if you let the first train go by in the hope of a seat in the next one? What if you are accompanied by your elderly parents and crying children? What if you are tired and do not want to travel standing? Or when you feel that you can get in but your bag cannot? Or when you want to avoid the long queue?

In all these situations, do you go home or do you simply stay on and wait for the next train?

There will be many metro situations in your business. And you don't have to ever give up, even if you miss many of these trains. There may be delays, situations may not be to your liking. But haven't you heard? Better late than never! So wait patiently and your time will indeed come.

Identify the situations in your business where things are not moving at the pace that you desire. Are you facing issues with timing? There can be multiple delays due to multiple reasons. Rest assured and show some perseverance. Remember, going back home has never been a solution and will never be one.

Soon, a metro train will arrive in which there will be sufficient space for you to sit comfortably and also fit in all your luggage and bags. Of course, there will be no crowds or queues. Yes, this train will be comfortable for old parents and children. Occasionally, your business will provide you with many such desirable turns to enter new fields. All you need to do is get to the platform, then stand and wait for your metro train—be mentally prepared to strike at the right time! Remember, 'Luck favours the prepared mind!' So, be prepared to grab your turn in business.

THE TIDE WILL TURN

21

BUSINESS AND A CRICKET MATCH

Let us take some time to watch a thrilling cricket match between the cricket teams of India and the West Indies at the world-famous Melbourne Stadium in Australia. The day is extremely cold as January is coming to a close. The stadium is packed to capacity; nearly 1,00,000 enthusiasts are expectantly watching.

Sachin Tendulkar, a talented Indian batsman, is batting on the field. He has already played fifteen balls, but he is not comfortable yet. On the other side is the renowned bowler Malcolm Marshall from West Indies. Marshall is towering at 5 feet 11 inches and is ready to bowl another 95 miles per hour ball to a much shorter Tendulkar.

Marshall bowls with determination. He must take this wicket; he must send Tendulkar back to the pavilion. As he bowls, all the fielders seem to be rushing towards Tendulkar. The environment is charged and competitive. The wicketkeeper must stump the batsman out at the earliest. All the fielders, including those on the boundaries, are ready to take a catch even if they have to stretch beyond themselves. The bowler is eagerly ready to take a catch if the ball comes his way.

There is hunger in the air.

On the other hand, the batsman is struggling. He wants to make his country proud. He is cool-headed and determined. The other batsman in the field reflects his endless energy and is ever prepared to take a run at the first available opportunity.

All the spectators supporting the Indian team want to see them win. They cheer. The Indian players in the dressing room zealously want India to win the match by a big margin.

In this cricket match, everyone is a competitor. West Indies is the competitor of India. The batsman is the competitor of the bowler in the match. The batsman is the competitor of the other batsmen of the country. He is also a competitor of the batsmen of his own team, desiring to make the most runs. Every bowler is a competitor of the other bowlers of both teams. This competition is also applicable to the fielders. If you take an even closer look, the spectators are competing with the other spectators spread across the world.

We are all similarly competing in our personal and business life. Although little reverence is attached to these words—competition and competitor—I find their inspiration in my personal and professional life. Competitors enhance the learning curve; they provide me with reasons to improve the business. Healthy competition fosters business growth.

When I see the 2,000 crore valuation of my competitor, I am motivated to work harder. I introspect about what is missing in my product, my service, my innovation and my thinking. I consider my own difficulties and challenges. My competitor ahead of me convinces me that there are higher levels to reach.

And if I would have already been the best, then I would make sure that no rival can catch up with me. To stay ahead of the pack, make your competitor your role model. Create a new recipe from the recipe of your competitor instead of copying him. Have faith in your abilities and add your own flavour or tadka to it. Believe me, this new recipe will be distinctive and will take you ahead in life. If you are lagging behind, then something is obviously missing. So you need to work on self improvement and take up new initiatives. However, are competitors absolutely necessary to motivate yourself? No. Competition is not required all the time. To constantly improve yourself in your performance, you do not need external competitors. You can be your own competitor. You can also motivate yourself by focusing on the journey and be prepared. But if you do have competition, you must face them. In today's world of cut-throat competition, the number of competitors can increase overnight. Many new competitors may be entering the market on a regular basis. But remember, their experience may be less than yours. And that clearly is to your advantage. If you have the advantage of being the first mover, you must also be prepared to face the next yield of competitors. Don't stress; be fearless face and fight your competitors. When you do so, you start your first move towards defeating them. Furthermore, it is a positive sign to have competition in business. Healthy competition leads to tremendous growth.

You can face and beat competition successfully only when you can identify the nature of the competition. The competition may be due to innovation or better marketing techniques. It could even be their discount policy or packaging. Identify all the potential threats to your business. You may even be lucky. You may be surprised to find that you were apprehensive of stiff competition when actually there was no competition at all.

We don't always think, understand and identify the factors that lead to competition. There may be hundreds of reasons. As an entrepreneur, your focus should not be limited to knowing about the competition but also on the factors behind its existence. Cricket matches are not always short like the 20–20 matches. Sometimes they are matches with fifty overs; at other times, they can be long Test matches. Similarly, you may find yourself in different competitive situations. Just remember that the competitiveness of your organization is viewed on the basis of many aspects, like your quality and competencies of human resources (HR), the number of business units, management of the supply chain, updated accounts and finance, process-based vendor management, robust IT, controlled SOPs and a lot more. Therefore, you must look at the managerial team of your competitor. This will help you do a detailed SWOT analysis. Making a list of these various components, you may find that you do not yet possess some of these desirable aspects. You do not need to fear entrepreneurial competition at all.

Digitization is the new word to compete in today's global perspective. Unfortunately, due to Covid-19, work from home became a necessity and for the first time ever we have seen a huge skill gap, not only at the organizational level but also at the employee level. There was a lack of digital infrastructure and digital literacy at various levels adversely affecting the survival of organizations.

Your organization and its employees must be digitally literate and continuously updated with the latest on the block. Moreover, are you yourself on the relevant digital platforms? Not only your brand name but also your employees can contribute a lot if they have digital competitiveness in the market.

Finally, develop a pragmatic approach towards competition and love it; you will see business growth. When you have courage, even ghosts run away. This is merely competition.

Strive to have create competitive advantage in your segment. View competition positively, remain vigilant and learn how to add value for the stakeholders.

STAY HUNGRY, KEEP AWAKE

22

WHERE DO YOU SLEEP?

Once, a businessman suffered a huge loss. This was partly because of peculiar circumstances, but mostly a result of critical mistakes he had made. As a result of his loss, the businessman was troubled. He was unable to decide whether he should restart his business or not. Deeply perplexed by this development, he even considered renouncing the world and leading the life of a sanyasi. His family members and well-wishers tried to help him find peace of mind.

Finally, after deliberations, he decided to spend some time in a monastery to seek some peace and tranquillity.

He spent many days in the monastery and religiously attended all the prescribed prayer, yoga and meditation sessions. He carefully listened to the various sermons.

Despite his efforts, he could not find convincing answers to his many questions. He couldn't find his way. Finally, he sought out the head priest at the monastery and asked him to help.

The priest considered his dilemma and said, 'Those who sleep on the floor never fall from their beds.'

Before the priest could elaborate, the businessman left from there. He drove away from the monastery, guilt about his business decisions plaguing him.

Unbothered by the businessman's absence, the priest continued, 'Life has its peculiar ways. It throws up many surprises, some are pleasant while others are not. We need to take them as they come and even in adverse situations, we must never give up.'

Twenty years ago, Indian businessmen followed the priest's aforementioned dictum. The priest at the monastery quoted it often. But much has changed. Over the last two decades, Indian businessmen have started to believe in a modified version of the quote.

'Why sleep on the floor when a bed is readily available?'

Let me explain this stance differently. Earning profits is the motto of any business. Every business must be financially sustainable—your earnings must be more than your expenses. In the modern business world, a number of businessmen have begun to accept that a new business will incur losses in the initial years. Earlier, this was only acceptable of capital-intensive industries, such as a steel plant or an oil refinery. Only these industries needed a gestation period of a few years.

Today, when setting off to operate a business, many investors are already prepared to support you. This is a clear shift. Traditional business families in India believed in the typical saying '*Pehle saal hatti, doosare saal chatti aur teesare saal khatti*', translated as, 'Devote the first year to investments in your new business, expect and accept some losses in the second year and expect to earn from the third year'. This was a popular and practical lesson for all entrepreneurs.

In the first year of operations, they needed to build a strong customer base and understand the market well. They had to make their presence felt, face competitors and competition in the market. In the second year of operation, they had to continue all of the above, even if there were operational losses. They still had to understand their customers and win them over. They would need to maintain the quality of their products or services and increase their product range. Apply the rule to your own business. If you are able to successfully do these things then you can expect profits to start pouring in during the third year of operation.

It is not necessary for all new businesses to incur losses in the first or second year of operation. However, businesses today need between two and five years to hit break-even point. Some may even have advantages like the ready availability of investors and easy scalability.

If you plan to start a new business in the mentioned category, ensure that you have adequate funds to last you till you achieve your break-even point. Your entire team must be motivated enough to see the interim or gestation period. Investors must be made available in case of any need. You must have proper secrecy mechanisms in place so your business interests stay protected during this period. You must obtain the requisite copyrights, trademarks and patents, etc. well in time.

You ought to draw up and follow weekly, monthly and yearly work plans. Make sure that the milestones that you wish to achieve are in writing to avoid any slips. You must have the SOPs in place as well as other preparations.

You will also need a Plan B. If your first plan fails or faces hiccups, your backup plan will come in handy. Additionally, you must be

ACCELERATE WISELY

prepared to celebrate your achievements time to time. Keep adding new milestones.

Even in the case of initial losses—year after year, quarter after quarter, month after month—your business losses must decrease. Further, this loss (also referred to as 'burnings') must reduce continuously. If that happens, once you achieve the break-even point it will not take you long to start generating profits.

It is your choice whether you subscribe to the old school or the new, whether you sleep on the floor or the bed. Your decision will largely depend upon your business idea, the specific needs of your business, the size of your pockets, availability of investors, your daring attitude, scalability of your business and other factors.

Decide your course of action after considering the nature of your product or service and the risk involved. Just in case you happen to face a failure, you must not consider it the end of the road. Don't head to a monastery to find your peace of mind. Instead, use your failure as a stepping stone to success—take the first step now!

23

ALL IS WELL IS NOT WELL

Once upon a time, there lived a man named Dinesh Kumar in a small Indian village. Dinesh was a god-fearing man who believed that everything happened because God had willed it thus. He was convinced that he had a special and direct relationship with his God and if he ever needed his help, God would be there.

One rainy season, unprecedented floods hit Dinesh's village. The water rose with every passing minute. Most of the villagers decided to leave the village and seek higher ground; they would return when the water receded. The sarpanch agreed. But Dinesh scoffed at the situation. He believed that things would get better since his God was looking after him.

Soon, the entire village was flooded. Most of the houses were devastated. Water was pooling in Dinesh's house. The state government had sent flood relief teams, duly equipped with rescue boats. They made announcements on their loudspeakers, urging people to immediately leave their houses. They announced that the water levels were expected to rise further during the next two days.

Dinesh was disturbed by these announcements. He wasn't sure if he wanted to leave his house at all. He said to himself, 'I shall not leave my house and go anywhere.'

Again he prayed, 'Things will go back to normal soon. My God is with me. I know how to swim.'

The very next day, the waters rose further. Alarmed by this, Dinesh moved to the roof of his house with whatever items he could carry.

As the floods worsened, helicopters with rescue teams were rushed to the village to save people. One by one, they airlifted those who were stranded on their roofs using rope ladders.

Dinesh watched. He thought to himself, 'I know it will get better within a day or two. God is with me.'

Duly assured, Dinesh neither waved to the rescue teams to seek help from the roving helicopters nor did he catch hold of any of the ladders sent for his rescue.

The same evening, gushing waters razed Dinesh Kumar's house to the ground. Unable to hold on to anything, Dinesh drowned. After his death, Dinesh Kumar faced his God. Dinesh cried bitterly, his faith shaken. He said, 'My Lord, You never came to help me in my hour of crisis. You did not rescue me. You allowed me to die. I consider you responsible for my death.'

The Lord smiled upon him. 'My son, I repeatedly came to you. I wanted to rescue you. I tried my best to help you. Despite my attempts, you did not listen to me at all! I first came as the sarpanch and your neighbours. The next time, I came to you in a rescue boat. I repeatedly shouted at the top of my voice and urged you to come with me. But again, you did not come.'

The Lord continued, 'I made one last attempt by coming to you in a helicopter. I even extended the rope ladder to you. But again, you never caught it. You chose to stay. You did not accept nor adapt to the situation. You are responsible for your death.' The constant series of events provided Dinesh Kumar with many options, but his single-minded belief (consciously or unconsciously) did not allow him to make the most of it and this led to undesirable consequences.

Change is the key, whether for success or doom.

Covid-19 has wreaked more havoc globally than the story of this flood. There is no way for businesses across different countries to have prepared themselves to face this situation. You might have heard about terminologies such as bringing a change, adopting change or change management. The Covid-19 era has somehow forced us to adopt and change, i.e., the new normal. This has taught us that if businesses will not be open to change with time, then they will be out of the business league. So we are all adopting and adapting to changes while realizing the pros and cons. Why can't we have a proactive approach towards change forever? Our organization must be ready with change management plans and welcome it as a culture. Analysis of these change management plans are equally important. It is recommended that you set quarterly or half-yearly 'change analysis approach' meetings in your company. Do some data analysis and compare the results with the short-term and long-term goals. Once you identify the scope of change on the basis of data analysis, start planning for it. Make the necessary changes within the organization from top to bottom to become future ready. If in the process of this change, any skill enhancement is required for staff/management representatives, just plan for it without a second thought.

For most businesses across the world, the pandemic has spelled closure or major losses. Some businesses were able to survive and fight the situation better than others. We now know that the businesses and businessmen were ready and quick to adapt to the changing scenario were the ones survived. Some other businesses even grabbed the new business opportunity brought about due to this emerging scenario. They were the ones that not only survived but benefited from the pandemic that killed many.

Businesses associated with manufacturing and/or marketing of necessary items like hand sanitizers and sprays, personal protective equipment (PPE) kits, safety shields, masks, digital infrared hands-free thermometers, cleansing products, faucets, automatic (sensor activated) doors, among many others were the primary beneficiaries of this boom. Those involved in these businesses were quick to respond differently to the ongoing crisis. Consequently, they gained from it. Some new entrants also benefited from the crisis. Many businesses made modifications in their existing businesses and survived the crisis.

Since all educational institutions were shut down—coaching, teaching and learning moved from the offline to the online model almost overnight, benefiting the companies already in this sector. Furthermore, the pandemic forced people to spend time indoors boosting the content creation and media sector. The entertainment industry which already had a foothold online saw a huge jump in demand. Suddenly, OTT (over-the-top) became a buzzword in the home entertainment industry and new rules had to be framed for this sector. Accelerated e-learning also gave birth to the homeschooling concept and hybrid learning products. Similarly, shops for groceries, vegetables, fruits, apparel, footwear, medicines and almost every other item witnessed a drastic drop while e-commerce platforms gained.

CHISEL YOUR THOUGHT INTO VISION

It is pertinent to note here that multiple innovations in different segments will be the stepping stones for many innovations in the next fifty years.

Let's be prepared to adapt and change. The sooner we adapt, the better for us. After all, God helps those who help themselves.

24

TO HELL WITH EXCUSES

Once upon a time, four friends decided to start a business. They were a lazy bunch, continually being reprimanded by their families who were tired of their lacklustre ways.

The four wanted to show the world that they too could become successful businessmen. They bought a second-hand taxi. Each day, the four of them piled into the vehicle—two in the front and other two in the back seat—and ran their taxi on the city roads looking for passengers. Each day, they would come home tired and grumbled that they had found no passengers despite their hard work. Within a few days, they squashed this idea.

Then they decided to open a car repair garage. They rented a large space on the first floor of a building and opened their garage. Daily they called out to people passing by but none came. They were confused and finally, after a long night of bemoaning their fate, they decided that the second-hand taxi that they had bought had been a bad omen.

They decided to throw the old car into the river. Two of them started to push it from the rear. The other two went to the front and started pushing it back. Their luck was bad, as they later said. The car obviously did not move a single inch.

After much deliberation, they reached a conclusion that their old ways had been right after all. All their hard work and energy had amounted to nothing in the face of bad luck. It would not allow them to succeed in any business venture. Do you agree with this hard-working lot and their logic?

When it comes to reasons for not doing something, I hear many different ones.

For example, I am fifty years old now and I have never travelled frequently and the business requires a lot of intercity and international travel. How can I do it now?

Or, for this kind of business, I need to open a shop in the crowded main market. It is nearly impossible to find a vacant shop there! Even if I can find one, the rent will be extremely high. How can I make any profits after paying such a high rent?

Or, what if I incur a loss in this business? How will I spend the rest of my life?

Or, this business requires a lot of capital. It will burn all my money.

Or, how can I open a dry cleaning service when I know that it runs during the winter months?

Or, I can't open a garment shop because trends change so quickly. I may be stuck with old-fashioned garments which I may never be able to sell. Isn't everyone looking for branded garments these days anyway?

Or, I can't open a saree shop! Sarees are old-fashioned. Aren't all the girls wearing jeans, T-shirts and trousers?

Or, businesses today involve too many lies and cheating and fraud.

Or, I'm not fit enough. I would have to wake up early in the morning and ensure the distribution of handbills and newspaper advertisements. The shop will have to be open on all seven days of the week, without holidays or rest!

Or, parking is such a big problem in the main market. No customer will come.

Or, these days you need to have good qualifications before you can start your business and I don't have them.

Or, businesses require employees and you cannot easily find honest and hard-working employees.

I have heard these and many many more. Each of these reasons surprises me. Indeed, those who look for excuses get them aplenty.

If you are interested in these reasons to explain away why you should not or cannot start your business, you don't need to think too hard. You will find them by the dozen. Concentrate on finding the reasons why you *should* start your own business. Those who do not want to do something, are always able to find reasons for not doing it. And those who want to do something, can always find many ways to do what they need to. Change your attitude and perspective and things will change for the better. This has been true for me on many occasions.

You will find that there are hundreds of opportunities and businesses that you can start with your abilities and education. Don't see your existing status or position as a hindrance to starting a new business. If you can see just a small little light at the end of the tunnel, believe that with time and hard work, you will soon be able to see plenty of sunshine. A human being can design his destiny; designing and starting a new business is much easier.

What are the reasons to do business?

Business makes you your own boss and puts you in charge of your future. Whether you are highly educated or not, you can excel on the basis of your experience and wisdom. When it comes to flexibility or time, your business will give you plenty. Increasing or reducing your profit margin is completely in your own hands. Your small starts will promise you phenomenal growth. Given the high consumption of various goods and services in our country, there are multiple opportunities in hundreds of fields. You also have the option to expand the same business or to diversify into a totally different field. When you are in business, you can be as creative as you want. A business provides you with opportunities to learn, unlearn and relearn while growing in more ways than one. A business knows no geographical limits. A business will help you derive personal satisfaction at the end of the day. A business may become your legacy. With the easy availability of funds, budgets do not limit a modern businessman.

Have you ever paid attention to understanding the psychology behind excuses? Do we make excuses in terms of having a fine dining experience even when the bill is to be paid by someone else? Do we make excuses when we want to go on a leisure trip? Do we make excuses to party? No, most of the time we don't. But when things take us outside our comfort zone or cause either physical or mental difficulty, we are likely to make excuses. That's where we need to train ourselves.

There is one easy way to practise it. Make sure to do something challenging every day to train your mind. It is just like developing or building one particular muscle of your body at regular intervals to get positive results.

You become capable of making the excuses you have often wished. These excuses can be both positive as well as negative. Please be positive towards your life and your business and look for positive excuses only.

A RAY OF EXCELLENCE IS ALL YOU NEED

There is a famous saying in India, '*dhoondne se toh bhagwan bhi mil jate hain, fir excuses/positive excuses kya cheez hain.*' This can be translated as: If God can be found, how difficult could it be to find excuses?

There are endless reasons to start one's own business. Find reasons for starting your own. Then look for ways to operate it efficiently. The pocket size of the buyer is increasing every day. Consumption patterns are also changing fast. A business that looks simple and average often has tremendous growth opportunities that lie hidden. Further, if you start your business now, there is every likelihood of your soon finding another business that would be complementary to your existing business and can be run alongside your original business. So, what are you waiting for? Get going. Your business is waiting for you!

25

STORYBAAZ

Let us visit a large saree boutique in a metropolitan city. We see sleepy husbands accompanying their wives and denying themselves a nap, daughters accompanying their mothers, party-goers and friends. They all have a single demand: 'Show us something that is trending.'

Typically, after spending some time talking to a customer and establishing a rapport with her, you could hear a smart salesman say, 'Madam, this is exactly the saree that Katrina Kaif wore in her latest film. As soon as the film was released, we rang our artisans in Benares and told them to come up with this replica. The original saree cost the producer ₹1,75000, our version will be yours for just ₹15,000. We had our own artisans in Benares make it. You will not get it at this price at any other shop. In any case, our fabric is far superior to the original. Here, try it.

What exactly is the salesman doing here?

The salesman has smartly shifted the onus of selling the saree to the celebrity, Katrina Kaif, making her his brand ambassador. If you were the customer, your focus would have shifted to this particular saree through this association.

To complement his first move, the smart salesman quickly takes out his mobile phone from his pocket, selects a particular picture and pops his mobile in front of you. 'Madam, look, Katrina Kaif is wearing exactly the same colour, print and embroidery.' And he zooms the picture to allow you to have a closer look at the similarities between the two sarees—in terms of their design, colour and embroidery. He is quick to add, 'Despite our orders, our artisans have only finished three pieces and they were delivered to us this very morning.'

Are you really left with any choice other than to go for this beautiful artwork in front of you? With his smart talk, the salesman now has also drawn the attention of the other customers in the store. One or two can be heard asking to be shown the same saree. Some storytelling indeed!

Here, I bring in storytelling. It is absolutely important to incorporate storytelling techniques in our businesses.

We are familiar with many stories, some loved and some tolerated, Panchtantra and Shakespeare, Akbar and Birbal, mythologies and personal histories. Films with a good storyline are the most successful. Stories narrated by our mothers and grandmothers in childhood had a lasting impression. They never grow old or boring. 'The universe is made of stories, not atoms,' said the famous poet Muriel Rukeyser. Stories are everywhere. When we watch a movie with our family, we enjoy those films the most that have a storyline. Family drama, tragedy, comedy, social message or anything else with a story to back them appeal to our senses and give us real joy. But storytelling is also an art and a skill. The storyteller, much like the salesman, is a practised artist. He sharpens his skills by observing what keeps his audience attentive specially when narrating stories to them.

Every business should incorporate an empathetic story into its communications with customers, suppliers, financiers, employees, partners, business associates or the masses at large. Humans are empathetic by nature. We respond to stories as stories allow our emotions to come to the fore; stories forge connections and enable dreams, and even assist us in making sense of our troubles. Stories can be viewed as techniques to counter challenging conversations where you are supposed to put across your viewpoint. It is a simple process. Just listen to the conversation and try to quote a story or even convert an incident into a short story! Be confident and try your best to show something while you tell tales to the person sitting in front of you. You will see that the other person will start relating to the situation.

A business with an empathetic and relatable story attracts and retains customers. Learn the skill of empathetic and relatable storytelling and add an element of surprise to these stories to make them enchanting. You will be able to build a direct connection and a trusting relationship with your customers.

Business stories can also be impactful. These stories can take your customers' experience with your product/service to a different height. By narrating delightful and authentic stories, you will be able to hold the attention of a buyer. Stories will help you build your brand and win your customers' loyalty—a certain way to enhance your profitability in the long run.

However, make sure that your story is honest and meaningful, rather than false and flimsy. Most importantly, your story should provide an insight into your business, product, brand, people and practices; an unrelated story will not serve the purpose. Start telling engaging stories instead of narrating the features and benefits of your product or service.

Make sure to centre your competitive edge.

It is a win–win situation. Your encouraging stories will keep your employees motivated, build goodwill, and add value to the lives or businesses of your customers/clients.

Be a good storybaaz.

A good storybaaz knows that he does not need to attract an audience through analysis or logic. He must focus on the hearts and emotions of the audience. Our mind sees a reason to connect when our brains produce the happy chemical called oxytocin, a 'feel good' hormone. We simply love to hear good stories that are well told. Biologically, our systems are built so as to connect with stories.

If you have not prepared stories of your business yet, then this is the right time. Start cooking your stories quickly and become a storybaaz.

COMPASSION DETERMINES COMMUNICATION

26

ONE THING AT A TIME

I recently attended the silver jubilee celebrations of my friend, Kanwaljeet Kohli, and his wife, Simran, of their anniversary. After the party, I thought about their enduring love. Kanwaljeet's history flashed before my eyes like a movie.

I met Kanwaljeet as a child. We were in the same class in school, we attended tuitions together and even helped each other learn and cheat in the examinations. After college, Kanwaljeet had taken a job and would commute to work in a public bus. Simran took the same bus to college, where she was in her final year. For Kanwaljeet, it was love at first sight.

He liked her and even hinted at his interest but Simran did not even acknowledge his presence. One day, Kanwaljeet told us—a group of four close friends—that he was determined to get married to her, despite not even knowing her name. He would get to it one thing at a time.

Putting our wits together we found out her name and her address, by following her home. To our surprise, she lived right behind Kanwaljeet's house. The two houses shared a common wall! That made things easy for my friend. He shifted to the room which had the common wall and soon convinced his father that he needed a window there, to let in fresh air. From there Kanwaljeet would gaze lovingly at Simran every day.

Kanwaljeet was smart and charming. He had learnt from Bollywood. *Padosan, Ek Dooje Ke Liye* and *Aamne-Saamne* were his inspirations. After a year of effort, Kanwaljeet and Simran grew closer and soon enough, the two of them fell in love. The two lovebirds kept their love and their meetings secret from their respective families even though they all knew each other.

At Simran's elder sister's marriage, Kanwaljeet took great pains to attend to all the sundry jobs. Simran made an attempt to impress Kanwaljeet's mother. Finally, Kanwaljeet and Simran took her elder sister into confidence and a proposal was sent across to Kanwaljeet's house. After initial resistance, Kanwaljeet's father too agreed to the proposal.

Only Kanwaljeet, Simran, her elder sister and the three of us friends knew that this was a love marriage and not one arranged by the respective families.

Kanwaljeet had been patient. Once he got to know where Simran lived, he was able to learn her name; once a window opened, he was able to get to know her better; once he was able to know and impress her, he charmed her; once they were in love, he was able to convince the families that they were an ideal match. Kanwaljeet's confidence that taking pains to move forward one thing at a time led to a miraculous matrimony.

Small- and medium-sized businesses can learn from him. In business, you should always tackle one thing at a time. This approach is applicable in many aspects of your business.

Begin by launching your products and services within your own state. This can be followed by spreading their reach to other states. Once you are successful, take them to the nation at large; your national success will open the door to take your products and services to the global level.

Additionally, keep innovating your products and services, year after year, one after the other. Your innovation should be launched one by one and not at one go. Your products and services are likely to lose their charm in absence of innovation.

Begin to advertise. Don't use all the mediums at once. Instead, test and trial every market until you are able to identify the best and the most effective medium.

Focus on the packaging. You will need to constantly improve—year after year, one improvement after another.

Inculcate a sense of responsibility in all your team members. You can increase or decrease these responsibilities depending upon their competence; with time, you can increase your dependency on them as well.

Ensure that the quality of your product is the best among all your competitors. Your product distribution channels should also be efficient. Similarly, you have to be ahead of your competitors in terms of pricing, feel-good factor and even profitability. Again, this should be done by following a stepwise approach. Attempting too many things at the same time may land you in trouble. They say to eat your elephant bite by bite, which simply means that even massive targets can be achieved when broken down into small chunks.

FAITH IN SUCCESS, SUCCESS IN FAITH

Furthermore, in every business you reach a stage where both forward and backward integration is achievable. In my opinion, attempt backward integration. It is relatively easier to plan and achieve backward integration and chances of failure are lower. However, if you can go ahead with both, consider backward integration first. Thereafter, you should go for forward integration, followed by backward integration and so on. As businessmen, we are always in a hurry and sometimes, this formula to attempt things singularly and one thing at a time may not really be possible. Even so, we must try to ensure that smaller chunks work before attempting the more cumbersome details. If you must, minimize the time spent between two things instead.

This stepwise approach will enable you to evaluate your own progress. You can then adopt more cost-effective techniques. This will essentially lead to higher profits and more progress. Remember, while you may be taking small steps your progress remains steady. It is a unidirectional movement towards growth.

You will also be able to reduce or remove unnecessary clutter which otherwise may impede your decision-making. You are now free to increase your footprint in other areas as well. Although this approach is time-consuming, it is a sure-shot way of achieving success in business. This is Kanwaljeet's way. Try it.

27

TUNE YOUR BUSINESS CLOCK

Bhavesh Aggarwal says that he wakes up every morning at exactly the same time as his mother in the adjoining room. Bhavesh is attached to his mother. Even when he is on tour, he calls his mother immediately after waking in the morning. His mother has a routine where she spends a few moments in meditation before leaving her bed. His phone is often answered by family members who inform him that she is chanting her morning incantations.

K.S. Kohli wakes up exactly at the crack of dawn. He has never set an alarm. His timing is so precise that even if the sun rises at 6.52 a.m. on a particular winter morning, my friend too wakes with the sun.

Why do these two men wake up with such precision? Do they possess supernatural powers? Are they unique? No. They have simply attuned their bodies to synchronize with nature.

Although we hear no ticking sounds, your body has a unique body clock that works on its perfect rhythm. It primarily regulates your sleeping and waking cycles over a twenty-four-hour period, naturally. This biological clock in your body is controlled by your brain, which sends the necessary signals to the different parts of your body.

If you sleep and wake at fixed hours, your body adjusts to keep those timings. You don't have to set any alarms. You will wake at a fixed time on your own. Even if you do set an alarm, your body clock is such that it will wake you up before the alarm rings. When it's time for you to sleep, your body will send the signals to cause sleepiness. Such is the precision of your body clock.

To make your business successful, always try to synchronize your body clock with your business clock. You will need to regulate yourself according to the demands of your business. You should only observe a Sunday when your business does the same. You should only punch out in the evenings when the business is winding down its activities. You should celebrate when your business does the same. And so on.

You must, essentially, tailor your body clock to correspond to the needs of your business. You must always be in the same time zone as your business clock, chalking out your plans in such a way that they are in alignment with the requirements of your business and not necessarily in alignment with your own personal comforts. This must be mastered in the initial few years of your business. More or less, it is just like a program where you give inputs and the desired outputs are achieved. Similarly, when you program your mind with inputs towards aligning your lifestyle to your business, the whole environment will start giving you the desired outputs. You get what you feed in.

The more you gain mastery over this, the more your business will prosper. It will streamline your business. Your business will become more productive, more efficient and result oriented. Gradually, these

A HUNGRY BUSINESSMAN NEVER SLEEPS

achievements will be instrumental in the attainment of success for your business.

During the initial years of my business, I managed to align my body with my business clock. I could not celebrate my own birthdays or those of my wife. We even missed many of our marriage anniversaries. If my business demanded that I be in a different town, miles away from my family on Diwali, I would be celebrating Diwali miles away from my home and my family. I was working according to my business clock. There were no compromises on that front.

As a businessman, you too must tune your mind, body and thoughts according to your business and its hours. You must continuously adjust your working hours as per the needs of your customers. You need to set up suitable alarms in the system after assessing the probable emergency situations that may arise in the business.

Keep updating the clock regularly. Make this into a routine exercise. Enjoy the transformation!

28

LEARN FROM THE MISTAKES OF OTHERS

This story is about a stunningly beautiful state, one that is well known for being one of the largest in area with the lowest population and vast energy resources. Yes, Alaska. It is the largest American state, located on the northernmost and westernmost corner of North America and is majorly uninhabited.

As the seventh largest subnational division in the world, Alaska's size is twice the size of the second-largest American state, i.e., Texas. Due to its wilderness, it is also known as the last frontier. Alaska is a fantastic state that is also well placed geographically. It is the only state bordering Canadian territory and the Pacific Ocean. This territory is home to incredible species of animals. It is one of the most popular tourist destinations in the world with 1,800 islands, 3,000 rivers and more than three million lakes.

Furthermore, Alaska has huge oil and gas reserves and thus exports it to other parts of world. However, its other exports include seafood, primarily salmon, cod, pollock and crab. The cost of living in Alaska is high, but people still prefer to move there due to its beauty, affordable real estate, lowest taxes, the possibility of adventure, hunting and fishing, the round-the-clock sunshine in the summer and much more. Here, employment is largely in the government and industries, such as natural resource extraction, shipping and transportation. The state has the longest coastline as compared to other American states. There is a lot to explore, from national parks, artefacts, museums to fairs and a rich history.

Interestingly, Alaska became an American state formally on 18 October 1867. When we see the history, America acquired Alaska from Russia. On one side, Americans were very optimistic about the deal considering it as a road map to expand American trade in Asia. In contrast, Russia could not anticipate the tremendous potential in Alaska and consented to such a deal. Hence, the purchase of Alaska was made at a cost of $7.2 million (approximately) at the time. Undoubtedly, the territory added lakhs of square miles to the United States, but America benefited many times more than what it paid. After the purchase of Alaska, America discovered many gold deposits in the region. Giving away Alaska, Russia lost many things, like access to natural resources like coal, molybdenum, platinum, and natural gas and sources of income through tourism, exports and more. Alaska is one of the reasons that the United States of America has emerged as a superpower in the world. Today, Russia regrets it and calls this decision a big mistake.

As humans, we are also meant to make mistakes. Yes, it is true that every mistake teaches, but another truth is that if we continue to learn only by making mistakes, learning happens very late in life. Let's know some common mistakes made in the business fraternity and derive our learnings from them.

Not giving first priority: Even today, business is not our first priority mainly because we Indians don't consider it a skill-based job, a full-time career or a lifetime earning source. This is the reason we don't start business in the first go. We keep lots of options open. It is commonly seen that when we are not able to pursue career paths in professions like medicine and law or secure government jobs, then we are more inclined to go into business. Later, when one steps into business, there is a casual approach because it is considered as the last resort. We don't tend to complete our business studies to gain subject knowledge and basic insights. Similarly, we don't pursue any internships or industrial training that can boost our skills. Later, when business demands technical knowledge to remain competent in the market, we become restless because the prerequisite skills have not been learnt by us.

No focus on team building and evaluation: Another commonly seen mistake is that we either don't form a dedicated team or are late in doing so. However, a team plays an important role towards achieving goals faster. Nowadays, workforce dynamics have taken a new shape; you need to build your team keeping in mind the future of the organization at large. A business suffers when we try to do everything on our own. As a result, success comes late or doesn't come even in the case of good businesses. Sometimes, when we have a team, we take time applauding the performer by giving promotions and bidding the underperformer farewell. We need to understand the relevance of team building and timely evaluation in order to implement our planned goals. Remember 'team works'!

Judgement without data analytics: Surprisingly, another big mistake we commit is relying more on our instincts than making data-based judgements. We must take a deep dive into subjects of concern like customer acquisition cost, cost analysis, best practices in industry, future projection, competitor analysis and more. In order to work on costs and analysis as a regular practice, we must take it step by step. You must collect data while providing goods or services. Make it a process to automate the collected data. Once your data is organized, plan to undertake data analysis using data analytical tools.

Lack of understanding about the power of pricing: Businessmen fail to understand the critical role of pricing in the success of business and invite downfall with inappropriate pricing decisions. Price is the foremost consideration for many customers and forms the first impression. The right pricing determines the future of your product and service. It involves calculated planning after market research and after checking your competitor's pricing. Pricing is a flexible element, so remember that both underpricing and overpricing are not favourable; it can either enhance the business portfolio or prove to be detrimental for the business.

Little documentation: In India people rely more on oral commitments and internal faith and have maintain less documents out of traditional practice (and ignorance). Your business documentation must be strong and capable of narrating the true picture. Build a robust document management system and safe-keep documents, like legal agreements, MoUs (memorandum of understanding), insurances, SoPs, compliance records, ownership records, government procedures, etc. It is recommended to keep documents digitally and backup your data regularly.

Not understanding the relevance of digital transformation: Many businessmen are not active on social media platforms (like Facebook, YouTube, Instagram) and have no business accounts. This is their biggest mistake as they lose connection and customers. These social platforms are powerful tools for brand communication, to reach one's target audience and to pitch for products and services and also to create awareness on the latest updates. Please don't ignore social media as you can bond well with your potential customers, providing convenience and personalization. You can get huge business recognition and connect with your clients within seconds of posting advertisements. Regular effort and the right content can help your business grow even with a small budget, increasing your return on investment (RoI) and making business competitive.

Small canvas: Another mistake commonly made by many business leaders is having a narrow vision. Businessmen must be far-sighted and keep their canvas big to paint a bigger picture. You must consider long-term rewards and the consequences of your decisions and initiatives. When you have a big canvas, you are able to deal with your business challenges and meet the day-to-day business needs, keeping their ends in mind.

Intolerance to criticism: Businessmen don't understand the importance of constructive criticism. This is another mistake they make when they react badly to feedback and criticism. With inputs from clients, employees, suppliers and others, you can improve your products, services and support. Don't take it personally as this is just another stepping stone to business success.

Impatience: Most businessmen are impatient in their business routines; this complicates things and makes them take hasty decisions. This is also a common mistakes and reflects your mindset. Patience is also a businessman's etiquette. Don't make a rapid and hasty assessment of any business situation. You can learn patience from an actor; repeating and rehearsing prepare an actor to maintain their calm and perform the best. Whether it is film or media, actors undergo different types of rehearsals, from table reading to role discussion and combination rehearsing. Similarly, you can perform different techniques to practise patience and follow a more process-oriented approach. After all, good things take time.

Lack of delegation: Most businessmen are not organized in operations despite it being an important management function. You must delegate authority with responsibility. The culture of organizing must be extended to the business, its process, departments and its people in order to deliver efficiency and for your business to become successful. You can make the chain of command clear by defining the organization's structure. You should be increasingly organized in business and day-to day conduct. Delegation of work allows your mind to be free to think about the strategic growth of your organization. Moreover, it directly enhances the accountability of the employees, which can be beneficial at the time of performance analysis of your workforce.

Not planning enough for the future: Another common mistake made by many businessmen is not planning ideas, concepts, solutions or projects, and instead focusing on implementation. As a result, they lack preparedness and seek corrective action (instead of preventive measures) to bridge the gaps. Sometimes excessive planning and lesser implementation can be detrimental, but at times the situations can be reversed. However, mere implementation without planning in business certainly does harm.

MISTAKES ARE READY RECKONERS

Learn from these common mistakes and make sure not to repeat them!

Interestingly, the lock of success can be opened with many keys—provided that the keys are used at the right time! As a businessman, you need to decide which key will be appropriate and at what time.

29

EIGHT OUT OF TEN

Monsoons had hit Delhi in the month of July. Mr Iyer, a resident of Telangana, arrived to meet his north Indian friend, Nisha. This was not the first time Mr Iyer had travelled to Delhi for official business.

Nisha planned to meet Mr Iyer outdoors, and treat him with a special lunch. She identified one of the best south Indian restaurant chains operating in Delhi. Finally, after an hour of exercising, Nisha booked a table at a renowned restaurant in Connaught Place after waiting in the long queue.

Mr Iyer arrived on time and was pleased to meet Nisha. He seemed distracted, looking around every other second, observing almost everything through his lenses. Both friends exchanged greetings and discussed their work. Nisha gladly ordered delicious rawa masala dosa, idlis, vada and uthappam, along with tempting sambhar and coconut chutney. She wanted to ensure that Mr Iyer felt comfortable and would be able to enjoy his meal.

The restaurant was full and as busy as bee. People rushed in like a swarm of bees, and left like a herd of deer to sample these authentic meals. In a couple of minutes, the feast for the day arrived.

Undoubtedly, Mr Iyer was hungry after a tiring journey. But he still took a moment to smell the aroma of food, just like a food inspector. Nisha noticed her friend doing so and was puzzled. Next, Mr Iyer took a spoon to taste the sambhar. Soon after tasting, a downward curve appeared on Mr Iyer's face. He was frowning. He started cribbing about the taste and the quality of the sambhar served to him. He explained what the key ingredients that make up a good sambhar were, and he looked disappointed as he spoke. Nisha felt a little disturbed but finished her meal quietly. Mr Iyer could not eat well without a sambhar of his choice. Seeing this, Nisha decided to take him to the famous Karnataka Bhawan, which was nearby (as per Google Maps).

The curving frown changed to a smile in no time. Mr Iyer was happy and hopeful now. This time, Nisha did not order anything for herself. Mr Iyer placed the orders. Again, there was silence until Mr Iyer picked up his spoon to taste the hot sambhar, which smelled good even from a distance. This time, he was speechless. He was not able to give it a ten on ten and started to look for gaps in the preparation. In this process, the lunch hour almost passed, though people continued to eat and arrive to dine.

Finally, Nisha broke her silence. With conviction, she told Mr Iyer that he would not be able to get anything in one plate in terms of taste, quality, texture, etc. She counselled Mr Iyer against comparing the meal prepared at a restaurant with food cooked by his own mother. She added words of logic and murmured, 'You have been eating food cooked by your mother for more than thirty years, how can you find a similar taste elsewhere? Settle for this, especially if the food is well cooked for the most part.'

She made it clear that the restaurants were cooking at least close to perfection while catering to thousands of customers on the daily basis.

The story of Nisha and Mr Iyer contains important business teachings.

At times, perfectionism leads nowhere. As seen in the case of Mr Iyer, it may lead you to starve for a day or to skip lunch. Similarly, a human being constantly looking for perfection sometimes stands at no man's land—in the process of attaining perfection, he may grow fearful of failure, and this ultimately decreases his ability to take a risk. Once that ability is suppressed, it also leads to a lack of creativity because they will not want to experiment or try anything new. Hence, in business, you should not crib or feel sad when situations are not meeting the mark—a ten on ten. Sometimes in the process of waiting for the best, you lose the more significant things.

In 2004, I was building my preschool franchise network pan-India. This involved travelling to different areas, to different nooks and corners of the country. Over time, I realized that with a change in geography, there is a change in language, tastes, preferences and also demand. It is very difficult to meet the needs and requirements on a ten-on-ten scale, specially when services are meant for everyone in the country. Again, you may be eight on ten in one region, while in the other you may be ten on ten, far exceeding the clients' expectations. Based on my personal experiences, I recommend that even a score of eight is a good number to achieve. I learnt that when quality education reached the Tier II and Tier III sectors of India for the first time, stakeholders gave an excellent response, while in metropolitan cities achieving a score of eight was tough.

A benchmark of eight on ten is acceptable as an ideal win–win situation. The number eight works as a green signal for almost every flight waiting to take off, because the parameters of ten on ten vary as per individual choices. These choices are established based on the nature and nurture of an individual in different physical environments. Similarly, a businessman must close a deal with a client if projected earnings and cost are eight out of ten.

In the business, there are several instances that call for timely decision-making. If you wait for a ten-on-ten score, you are likely to miss the boat. For instance, when you are conducting a recruitment drive, it is good to hire the job aspirant when his skills, competencies and required experience pass the test and enable him to score an eight. To understand further, refer to the period of massive rises in Covid-19 cases in India. In this situation, when the Covid vaccine manufacturers presented their products (vaccines) to the government, they were passed after due checks on a scale of mostly perfect after considering them majorly safe and beneficial for public interest. Thus, prepare yourself for an eight, and believe me, eight is a good number.

Globalization and uncertainty demands being flexible in the business environment, where things are changing beyond the expectations of businessmen. Now, we have to become flexible so that adaptability can be achieved. If you look at the current scenario, willingly or unwillingly we have changed ourselves and our way of doing business. Therefore, leaving perfectionism behind can readily assist us in becoming adaptable and dynamic in nature, which will ultimately make us sustain in the market.

If you are not conducting your business because you find it easier to complain, again and again, waiting for hundred per cent perfection, then it is not right. All qualities cannot be found in one business option. So please don't wait for a hundred per cent score or perfection in

CELEBRATE YOUR 99 AS MUCH AS 100

anything. Don't consider ten-on-ten as the single best outcome. Instead, I have been celebrating this number since an early age (and yes, my birth date is also eight). It is just a number and I am happy about it. After achieving a score of eight, I have never failed.

Remember that you are leading a business and your time is your most important resource.

So clear your mind with priorities and don't get stuck on tasks or projects for perfection. A quote by Winston Churchill says, 'Perfection is the enemy of progress.'

30

AN ACCIDENTAL BUSINESSMAN

I am an ardent fan of Dr A.P.J. Abdul Kalam, former President of India, and have turned to his books often. As a rule, after every general election, the President appoints the PM of the country from the party with the highest number of members of Parliament in the Lok Sabha. Such a process can be complicated when no single political party has a clear majority. In 2004, the year he was President, the general elections were in a similar quandary, with no political party having the strength to form a government on its own.

The Congress held the largest number of seats in the Lok Sabha. Despite this majority, for three days, no political party or coalition of political parties came forward to form the government at the Centre. Finally, the President's office had to take charge, sending a letter to the leader of the Congress, Sonia Gandhi, to come forward and stake their claim.

Mrs Gandhi scheduled a meeting with the President for 12.15 p.m. on 18 May 2004. But instead of arriving alone as she was expected to, she brought along the well-known economist Dr Manmohan Singh. She informed Dr Kalam that she had the requisite numbers and would come with the letter/s of support the next day. At Dr Kalam's request, she agreed to meet him the same day instead, at 8.15 p.m.

Within the office, debates raged. The President and his office were being urged not to appoint Mrs Gandhi as the PM of the country under any circumstances. Dr Kalam did not know whether that would be legally and constitutionally tenable. If she laid a claim, Dr Kalam would have had to appoint her to the position of eminence.

At 8.15 p.m. that evening, Mrs Gandhi presented the letters of support from the various parties to the President. After due process, she was advised that the President's office was ready for the swearing-in of the new PM. At this juncture, Mrs Sonia Gandhi told Dr Kalam that she would like to nominate Dr Manmohan Singh instead, a trusted lieutenant of the Congress party.

Finally, Dr Manmohan Singh's swearing-in ceremony took place on the 22 May 2004, in the Ashoka Hall of Rashtrapati Bhawan. He had a cabinet of sixty-seven ministers. After the ceremony, Dr Kalam heaved a sigh of relief; this critical task had finally been successfully seen to its end. However, he remained puzzled about why no political party had staked a claim to form the government for three days prior to this appointment.

Years later, Sanjay Baru, PM Manmohan Singh's media advisor from May 2004 to August 2008, published his memoirs—*The Accidental Prime Minister*—in 2014. The 2019 film, *The Accidental Prime Minister* is based on these memoirs.

Since then, the word 'accidental' has often been used in reference to

Dr Manmohan Singh. Similarly, there is a world of difference between a businessman and an accidental businessman. It is commonly believed that all you need to start a business is some capital, some space for a shop/office and a product that you can either manufacture or trade.

In business families, every young boy is nudged to get into business. Unfortunately, business becomes a default option for some. This default movement to business leads to the production of many accidental businessmen every year. Despite the requisite capital, rented or owned office space, a good enough product and other resources, many such accidental businessmen will never be successful. A report by the IBM Institute for Business Values and Oxford Economists found that 90 per cent of Indian start-ups fail within the first five years of operations. The primary fault is ignorance. Business is mostly seen as a lucrative option that attracts many. Print and electronic media have showcased businessman as well dressed, wearing corporate suits, expensive goggles, dining with clients at the finest restaurants, travelling by air and partaking of other such luxuries. These things create a positive idea of the businessman in the minds of people. Consequently, they make impulsive decisions and become accidental businessmen. Being a successful businessman involves a journey over a course of time, some planning, some sacrifices too.

It is good to be in business, but do so only after being aware of the journey of a businessman. You will have to face many struggles.

Most accidental businessmen do not realize that they first need to train themselves to conduct a business; when they fail, they tend to blame market conditions, government policies, their timing or destiny. You must learn to swim before actually jumping into the sea. It is time we broke free from this misconception and consider the prerequisites for starting a new business.

Times have changed and today conducting a business has become a challenging task. Competition has skyrocketed, globalization has changed the rules and the digital era has opened up a plethora of options. These factors make it almost impossible to operate a business without any training.

Becoming a businessman by default, an accidental businessman, is like buying a lottery ticket. The chances that lady luck will smile on you are minimal. Despite your investment of time and effort, you may never hit the jackpot. Instead, take the harder and well-trodden path. Do your research properly and train well before taking the plunge. We have access to the best resources, even in India. Various diplomas, degrees, short-term courses, internships are available. Well-established colleges, universities and other institutions are flourishing in both the government and private sectors.

I strongly recommend that you first understand the nitty-gritty of doing business and undergo suitable training before you jump. And if you have already begun operations, you must consider honing your skills.

WRITING YOUR DESTINY IS NOT ENOUGH, MAKE IT PRECISE, CLEAR, BOLD AND STRONG

31

CONNECTING THE DOTS

In life we come across different situations some of which look bright but do not materialise despite many endeavours. I believe that these half unfolded possibilities decode with time. I consider them as my life dots which shall connect in future. After taking you through the life journey of Steve Jobs, I will make you understand how I connected my life dots.

16 October is observed as Steve Jobs Day in California in honour of Steven Paul Jobs, also known as the 'father of the digital world'. Steve Jobs was not only a far-sighted technology expert, but also the co-founder, chairman and CEO of Apple Inc. Steve always followed his heart and intuition in whatever he did. He considered situations and experiences as dots that needed to be connected for a reason.

Steve grew up in an average working-class family with limited finances and was homeschooled by his mother in his childhood. He was exposed to mechanics at a very early age by his father who taught him how to build radios and televisions in their family garage. After completing high school, Steve chose to attend Reed College in 1972, despite the fees being as high as that of Stanford. Within six months of college, he dropped out; he didn't consider it valuable enough to spend his family's savings. After sometime Steve started to focus on his areas of interest and, joined again for the next eighteen months before he really quit.

Reed College had the best calligraphy course in the country at that time. This is where Steve pursued creative classes and learnt calligraphy to perfect an artistic form of letter writing. He was fascinated when he learnt about serif and sans-serif typefaces, about varying spaces between different letter combinations and what makes typography good. Calligraphy was beautiful to him, and while he knew that there it had no practical application in his life, he considered it a dot that would connect long dot some day.

Similarly, he did not have a room on campus, and he managed to sleep in a small space with his friends. After his parents requested that he go to Brandywine, which was not his choice, he found his best friend and identified what he wanted to do with his life.

Steve believed that only by looking backwards could one connect the dots.

At his first job, Jobs worked as a video game designer at a company and he created circuit boards for video games till 1974. But within two years, Jobs founded the Apple computer company with his best friend, Wozniak, and they sold circuit boards to their clients. In 1985, his life lost its balance. This is when Jobs left Apple due to disagreements between him and the CEO. He was fired from his own company. It was difficult for him to let go of what he called the focus of his life. Steve did not overthink this obstacle and instead focused on new projects.

In 1997, the dots were connected when he joined Apple again as the CEO and was able to rebuild their broken brand image.

In 2007, Steve released a new product called the iPhone. It was the first touchscreen phone. In 2010, he introduced the iPad, which he considered 'the biggest thing'. Steve's dots were connected when his former calligraphy classes helped inspire one of Apple's most important features. When Steve was designing the Macintosh computer, the calligraphy he had learnt ten years ago came back to him. This is the reason Mac was the first computer with such beautiful typography, multiple typefaces and proportionately spaced fonts. Steve continued to connect many small and big dots in his life.

Similarly, I too want to share about the major dots of my life, dots which have been connected in time. However, a few dots still remain. I don't know which of the remaining dots will connect and how, but I am sure time will unfold the event some day. Based on my personal belief, I can say that when these dots do come together, they will take a different shape or form a unique design. Sometimes they make a beautiful line and with time, these lines make a beautiful picture. Sometimes they make circles, squares and even random other shapes that I don't understand or take time to understand. Let me take you through the experiences that connected these various dots:

First Connection: When I was just fifteen years old, I was charmed by the idea of dealing in the share market. Somehow, I managed to invest in shares anonymously. Dematerialization of shares had not been introduced in India and the huge systemic gaps made my path easy. The physical forms required basic minimum information of the investor and I was able to proceed by inflating my age. I followed my heart and in approximately two years I had invested in the initial public offering (IPOs) of more than hundred companies. I did not reveal my interests to my family and was soon engaged in other ventures. Coincidentally, after ten years, I took the sub-brokership of the Delhi Stock Exchange and continued this old hobby as a business. This is when my first dot was connected and I felt like everything happens for a reason.

Second Connection: I was married at the young age of twenty-four and soon after, I gifted my self a one-year-long computer training course at a neighbourhood computer training centre. At that time, learning from private institutes was trendy and PCs' were too new as an accessory. I was very enthusiastic about this course, but all my dreams were shattered on joining the institute. Their computer systems, software and even their study material were too old and not up to date. The facilities, course content and the teachers were just average. I was not convinced about the teaching and learning practices and despite paying the total course fee, discontinued the classes in three months. I felt that I could run a much better computer training institute of my own. This is when the seeds of entrepreneurship were sown in me. This was my first step in the education sector and I had no regrets about my decision. The dots were connected when I started my very own computer training institute within two months of leaving the computer classes. Unconsciously, this was the start of a long innings in the education sector.

Third Connection: When I saw the preschool bookset of my daughter for the first time, I felt like I had been cheated. Surprisingly, there were only one or two books there. I remember that she had a pink book to study from for a period of two years in kindergarten. This is when I was motivated to do the homework and make sure my daughter's education was more reliable and more justified. Unfortunately, in some time, my smooth-running business of shares and my father's twenty-year-old export business were on the verge of closure. This is when my insights and learning in the playschool segment marked a new beginning and I connected the dots by founding the Bachpan preschool.

Fourth Connection: One day, I went to MM University for the admission of my daughter into MBBS. I closely saw the infrastructural facilities, professional practice, communication style, their schools with varied streams. Within moments, I was deeply encouraged by the sight of the same university—I wondered that if someone like me, someone from a non-academic background could do magic single-handedly twenty-five years ago, then I had already had a foot in the education segment for over fifteen years. This realization resulted in the foundation of Rishihood University with a themed education for impact. Rishihood is operational with world-class infrastructure at Sonepat in Delhi-NCR and focuses on building creativity, entrepreneurship and leadership in the students.

Fifth Connection: I went to get an MRI (magnetic resonance imaging) done since my leg had been giving me trouble. This is when I realized that there was tremendous scope in the medical field, especially in the wellness segment. This dot connected when I launched Delhi's biggest diagnostic centre, Must & More, in the year 2012. The facilities include a wide range of services like radiology services, pathology service/testing and nuclear medicine, along with all other routine checks. My motto behind its opening was to create a state-of-the-art centre that awed all my customers. Having worked in education, healthcare is another greenfield area that I entered.

Sixth Connection: I suffered from an attack of polio at the age of nine months. I started walking for the first time at the age of thirteen using calipers; this continued for thirty-three years. I have been on a wheelchair for the last five years. Soon after a shoulder injury, I was bedridden for six months. This is when I longed for accessible vehicles, an accessible built environment and even accessible pathways. I decided to take initiatives towards sensitizing people about the needs of people with disabilities; this led to the rise of the Hum Honge Kamyab Foundation. This phase became a turning point in my life. It changed me completely. Now I was able to understand the need for accessibility from the ground level. Because of this transformation, Rishihood University was built as per inclusive design guidelines. Today I feel happy that a school of para sports is in the making within Rishihood University.

Seventh Connection: Soon after my style class 12 examinations, I took a six-month-long journalism course, conducted partly through correspondence and partly through weekend classes. This is when I realized my love for writing, but I did not know the future of this interest. After five years, I got a chance to work with a small newspaper of the time. In two years, I started handling the responsibilities of co-editor. This is not all, at the age of fifty-one, I continue to write about my experiences, stories, motivational thoughts and more. The journalism course, followed by my experience with the newspaper, gave birth to a profound writer within me.

When I look back, I realize that these are some of the biggest dots that were connected. Yes, there are several other small dots which too were connected with time.

Similarly, being in business, it is your responsibility to make your dots consistently connect. At the same time, you need to have faith that your dots will some day come together. Sometimes, it is better not to evaluate situations and difficulties. Everything happens for a reason. You should not be pre-decisive or judgemental and wait for your dots to connect in the near future.

Dots not only make you aware of options, but they train your mind to work through uncertainties. You learn something from every dot—either tangible or intangible, both—they act as a mental exercise, leading you to become a sharp businessman. Nothing goes to waste in the business world, it all leaves an impression, directly or indirectly.

Whenever you feel disappointed tell yourself to wait for the right time. Believe that your unfulfilled dreams will get fulfilled one day. Be willing for connecting the dots in future. No one else will do this for you.

YOUR EXPERIENCES ARE YOUR PRIMARY COLOURS WITH WHICH YOU PAINT EVERYTHING IN LIFE

32

VOWELS OF A BUSINESS

Let us think about vowels. They are literally a part of languages, and figuratively a part of our culture and our business.

Vowels provide sound and shape to a word. They are an integral part of communication and they help us talk. 'A', 'E', 'I', 'O' and 'U' are vowels in the English language. Interestingly, vowels are important in many languages and are found in every syllable. Their relevance appears on the surface when we have to distinguish between words like slip and slap, clip and clap, cut and cot, etc. When children don't understand vowels, they struggle to develop reading skills.

Let's learn about eminent personalities who have become much like vowels in their respective segment due to their X factor, dedication and continued hard work.

The actor Amitabh Bachchan is a vowel in the film industry. He is known as the 'Guru of Indian Cinema', the 'Shahenshah of Bollywood', the 'angry young man', 'senior Bachchan' and as 'Big B'. The world admires him as an actor, a film producer, a television host, a playback singer and an influential personality. He has been honoured by the Padma Shri, Padma Bhushan, Padma Vibhushan and with the Dada Saheb Phalke Award.

Sachin Ramesh Tendulkar, the former international cricketing star, is a vowel in the Indian cricket fraternity and a global icon. The extraordinary batsman holds the record for most hundreds in both tests and ODIs. He is regarded as a genius cricket icon and is worshipped. He could score all around the wicket, off both front foot and back. He could tune his technique to suit every condition and made runs in almost all matches in different parts of the world. The little master made his debut at the age of sixteen and retired at forty with enthusiasm and pride.

Ratan Tata, the former chairman of Tata Sons, is a vowel in Indian business. His roots originate in a Parsi family, which has been in business since British rule in India. The businessman played a major role in raising the standard of the common man in India and has made India incredibly proud. Under his direction, the Tata group acquired major divisions like Tetley, Jaguar, Land Rover and Corus. Ratan Tata managed to make Air India profitable when it was sinking. He improved the financial state of Tata industries and due to his leadership, the company earned worldwide business successes.

Lata Mangeshkar, the outstanding playback singer, is a vowel in the music industry. She is known as the 'Nightingale of India', 'Queen of Melody', 'Voice of the Nation' and 'Voice of the Millennium'. She has sung songs in around thirty-six Indian and foreign languages, primarily in Marathi, Urdu, Hindi and Bengali. Since the beginning of her career in 1942, she has sung for nearly a thousand Hindi movies. The versatile singer has sung for actresses from Madhubala to Priyanka Chopra. Due to her achievements, she has been honoured with the Padma Bhushan, Dada Saheb Phalke Award, Padma Vibhushan, Bharat Ratna—India's highest civilian honour, Legion of Honour and other prestigious awards in her long career.

If you watch closely, then you will see vowels in varied segments. Similarly, you must become a vowel of your own business segment. As a businessman, make your presence count.

With some contemplation, you will discover that your business needs vowels. In the same way that vowels contribute to the development of a language and help in building a complete vocabulary, your business too needs its vowels. These vowels could be the vision and mission of your business (however, these are not considered important by many businesses and businessmen). These vowels could be quality standards pertaining to your products and services, transparency or commitment towards stakeholders. They can happen to be futuristic planning and expansion based on the type of your business. Sometimes these vowels can be your passion, perseverance and socio-economic impact.

Even though there are only five vowels in the English language, they form its entire basis. Sometimes, your patience, consistency and speed can become the vowels of your business. Every businessman should not only understand the vowels of his business but also become an architect of those vowels, and on the basis of this creation, he should decide the path for the business.

Be an outstanding team leader who knows his vowels. This will help you to achieve more and enable you to break boundaries that may exist within or outside you. Your initiatives as a businessman, in transforming lives and in business, will make you an unforgettable and celebrated icon. Please don't wait for consonants from A to Z. Achieve

YOU ARE SUCCESSFUL WHEN OTHERS SAY YOU ARE

the business vowels and gradually they will become your life.

Every business is capable of creating its own new dictionary, its own language and its own vowels. I have immense faith that your business has lot of potential. It is, however, relevant for you to understand how to go about it.

BE A BUSINESSMAN WITH YOUR OWN VOWELS.

33

THE GOLDEN CIRCLE

In the Indian context, consider why the Board of Control for Cricket in India (BCCI) was constituted under the jurisdiction of the Ministry of Youth Affairs and Sports, Government of India.

The role of the BCCI is that of a governing body. It looks after the day-to-day affairs of the Indian cricket industry. The board comprises many state cricket associations, mainly made up of ex-players, and these players select their representatives and elect a BCCI chief. Most importantly, when cricketers in India have to represent the country at various levels, a committee of cricket administrators under the BCCI is entrusted with the task of team selection for Test matches, ODI (one day international) matches and T20I matches in different parts of world.

To set the road map for success, the selectors look for the right combination of batsmen, bowlers, all-rounders and wicketkeepers in different matches. Age is not a criterion for team selection but capability to perform is of utmost importance. The arrangement of each team differs from format to format.

For instance, in a limited overs match, like ODI and T20I, it is important to select cricketers who have more than a few qualities. Hence, in a team of eleven players, we see a combination of four batsmen, three all-rounders, one wicketkeeper and three bowlers. On the contrary, we see a composition of five batsmen, one all-rounder, one wicket keeper and four bowlers in test cricket matches. Similarly, who will open the innings as an opener or who will bat as middle order batsman or who will be the finishers batting in the later stages of the innings is predetermined. The selectors have specialized knowledge and experience, and they decide the number of fast bowlers and spinners in the team as per the requirement. They know that all-rounders are highly valued players as they can play the role of two cricketers simultaneously. The idea is that with the right blend of players, the Indian team can perform well under varied circumstances. The board tries to balance youth and experience in each team. For instance, we have seen good bowlers in the South African cricket team, so the strategy is to have a good number of batsmen to balance team structure. Additionally, the composition of the opponent's team is equally important in deciding their own team's structure.

Indeed, the right mix of individuals in a team is important, but cooperation and coordination among the members also play a critical role. BCCI considers every player in the team important and motivates them to perform well at the time of matches. It looks at the task of team selection as a strategy to win any match. It hunts for the best cricketers based on their performance for inclusion in the Indian cricket team. I believe that the BCCI's team selection criteria can be followed by Indian businessmen to build their own team in an intelligent manner.

In any business, the choice of a team plays a significant role. I know you are aware of the terminology that is 'team building', but I would like you to consider it a little dynamically. You should weave your team structure as per the requirements of your business. The idea is to make a competent team, which can then be adjusted to work in any business-related format. You must plan and design the type of departments, the number of people, the kinds of people and the kinds of competency beforehand.

It is good to design KRA (key responsibility areas) for different roles and also for each department. A team should be chosen considering whether the team member is hard-working, dedicated and honest to take your organization to the next level. Remember, you can compromise on education, but not on the integrity of a candidate. When the team is decided, ask yourself, 'Do they have any role to play in your vision?' Identify whether these team members are with you for the short term or long term. I have generally seen that short-term candidates are not far-sighted and not able to gel with the vision of the organization, and vice versa.

The manner in which the team member can make a radical difference is difficult to anticipate in the beginning and can unfold over time. Organizations and leaders feel more confident when their skilled employees can adapt to the work rather than being hyper-focused on specific tasks. Don't forget to check the team's experience, comparing it to the role expected from them.

Fierce competition and digitization have raised the benchmarks of success. Something which was relevant a few months ago has become irrelevant by now. Similarly, the team has to remain relevant—either incorporate a new and talented workforce or start nurturing your existing workforce to improve their future employability.

Remember, a team which is aware, up to date and empowered works better and more efficiently your business goals. Such a team will not be at rest if there are any deficiencies in the system. If your team is with you and works with you towards attainment of common goals, then, my dear friends, the chances of your success become much brighter.

On the basis of my thirty-four years of experience in varied domains, I feel confident in making a strong statement: any person who is a master of a particular and individualized aspect will not be capable of being even an average businessman. You *must* be a team player to be successful. The foundation of any and every business is team spirit. Even a small business requires cooperation and coordination among its team members. Consider your stakeholders also as your team members who complete the golden circle of your business ecosystem.

Team utilization is as important as team building.

I am the captain of my team in my business. As a businessman, I am responsible for deploying my team to different grounds as per the need and time of emergency. Projected revenue from different sources decides the position of each team. I have broadly categorized my team on the basis of their skills, experience and competencies. This internal classification helps me make the right resource selection in order to implement the most viable projects and to deal with clients having high to low net worth. A business cannot be prosperous until the team members are made aware of their roles, responsibilities and operating fields.

It is perfectly okay if a team member is not engaged at any point of time. The idle time gives the team member time to polish his/her skills and acumen. Your junior staff should be engaged in handling miscellaneous tasks and related point of contacts. Similarly, business managers must be kept aside to deal with persons of their cadre. Senior management personnel in your organization must be engaged in high priority tasks and strategic decision-making. Some team members

TEAM + TOGETHERNESS = GROWTH

are the face of the organization and must be available at the time of corporate representation at eminent platforms and events involving stakeholders. This role-based demarcation brings efficiency to your business operations through optimum utilization of resources and it significantly contributes to business success.

Last but not the least, the powers and privileges given to the team must be in accordance with the value of that team member to your organization. Create your talent pool thoughtfully. This quality of team reflects the strength of an organization and demonstrates its preparedness for achieving its goals.

Weave the golden circle that shines bright. Add diversity to your talent pool and don't forget to nurture your team! As businessmen, you must learn the art of planning for the future and for retention too. The team has to be built, rebuilt and grown to achieve larger organizational goals.

34

QUICKEN YOUR BUSINESS

The story is about a fast-growing global Indian brand: Bharti Airtel. The communications giant has been quick to raise the bar as part of its mission while delivering best-in-class services to customers; it has been equally quick to learn from its mistakes, ensuring that they are not repeated. Similarly, Airtel has been quick to acknowledge its responsibility in providing access to high-quality telecom services, but also the responsibility of providing answers to all its service-related queries by responding and resolving them in a quick and transparent manner. In a short span, Airtel has evolved as India's largest integrated telecom provider and the second-largest mobile operator in Africa. It is the outcome of fast-thinking towards value creation for stakeholders and fast-advertising that Airtel has built one of the largest subscriber bases, connecting millions of people in India and abroad.

Airtel began its telecom journey in 1995 with the launch of cellular services but it had far-sighted vision. The idea was to conduct acquisitions and then enter into partnerships, expanding rapidly to other geographies. Thus, within two years of its foundation, a major UK-based telecom operator invested in the organization and in the fourth year, Airtel acquired stakes in leading cellular service operators in Karnataka and Andhra Pradesh and started operations in these two states under its brand. This was followed by the acquisition of many regional operators to increase its cellular network and then it rebranding them as its own. This is when Airtel showcased some speed.

Gradually, Airtel marked its entry into other markets, like Punjab, Uttar Pradesh, Maharashtra, Kerala, Gujarat and more, though IPOs and by winning the trust of its investors. Agile advertisement strategies helped Airtel become the largest private sector operator in a short period of time. Almost every year, different renowned personalities were made brand ambassadors while the organization launched creative offline and online campaigns. One of the greatest strategies adopted by Airtel to pace its operations was by outsourcing daily activities. Airtel partnered with organizations like IBM to outsource hardware, software and IT service requirements.

Presently, Airtel offers a gamut of products and services, including connectivity, data centre, cloud, cybersecurity, conferencing solutions and internet of things (IoT). Indeed, Airtel is fast in decision-making and in reaching untapped markets. When competitors were not even considering these options, Airtel already had the ball rolling and became the first operator to launch 4G in twenty-six villages located in the tough terrains of upper Ladakh. In 2011, Airtel introduced the first 3G service in India in the city of Bangalore and lakhs of customers had registered within seventy-two hours of its launch. Similarly, Airtel's

Payments Bank became the first payments bank in the country to go live as it rolled out services nationally.

Airtel continues to be a fast-moving brand that connect homes and touches millions of lives. This is possible because of its promptness in exploring potential markets, adapting new technologies, entering into strategic partnerships, innovative marketing and advertisement strategies and more.

Our small- and mid-sized business fraternity can learn a lot from these business giants and can build a road-map to accomplish growth, development and sustainability quickly. I believe that every business can become fast, but only on different parameters. It can either do so by making individual aspects faster, or by taking a combination of these aspects, be it technology, quality, products or solutions. It depends on the nature of the business activity. Which factors can contribute the most? Let's understand the different factors that help make your business fast:

Clarity on Vision and Mission: As a businessman, you know the purpose of your business and your strengths. So you need to brainstorm and draft the vision and mission statement for your organization, making sure that what you put across is unique, inspiring and attainable. Unfortunately, many businesses don't have vision and mission statements. Vision statements describe the desired future position of your organization, while a mission statement describes your business, its objectives and its approach towards accomplishing these objectives. Once you are clear on your vision and mission, everyone will be focused and dedicated to work towards a common purpose.

Quicker Decision-making: In business, you have to take both routine decisions and strategic decisions tactfully. Routine decisions don't require much analysis or in-depth study and must be taken under the fast-track route, while strategic decisions can have long-term implications and must be taken cautiously. Remember, every business needs a management that is quick in decision-making as this helps maintain a continuous work flow. Here, quicker decision doesn't imply decisions based on half-cooked information. Instead, these decisions must be quality decisions supported by due diligence and made only after considering the existing financial situation and relevant data. When you understand the difference between quick decision-making and incautious decision-making, you are able to avoid mistakes, implement policies, and timely respond to the customers' needs and the competitor strategies. Your time saved is time earned, and it is comparable to profit earned.

Accountability and Responsibility: You must try to bring accountability and responsibility into your business at all levels. It is better to have one candidate with principles such as accountability and responsibility instead of four half-invested candidates. Accountability is results focused and can be introduced as a culture through certain efforts, like providing clarity, training, fixing timelines, empowering the team; responsibility is task focused and can be introduced by rewarding, encouraging and leading by example. It is the role of the leadership to cultivate both these behaviour among fellow candidates. This will not only make your business fast but also reduce mistakes, cultivate perfectionism, increase self-esteem in employees and largely make your business healthy.

Decentralized Approach: Sometimes all your business planning, decisions, innovation, etc. is done in a centralized manner, which can delay the business. A decentralized approach works well to make your business fast. As a leader, you must decide on the factors that need to be centralized and the factors that can be decentralized; then you can adopt appropriate measures. This balance will bring speed to your business. Sometimes, centralized decision-making and a decentralized working approach is more effective to achieve one's goals.

Technology-driven: Technology can help you to work more efficiently. Automation can make your business agile and flexible. Bring in state-of-the-art technology and new tools to meet the needs of your business. You must explore different online products that help you make your business faster. Recognize the role of doing business on the cloud and digitize your data. Technology can be your business USP.

Data-based Decision-making: Don't jump to conclusions based on your instincts. Always make decisions supported by data analysis. This will make your decisions sensible and trustworthy in your future business efforts. Different tools are available to analyse different data sets depending upon the need. Your business insights can help you understand what kind of data is important for your business to reach the next level.

Be Experimental: Be flexible to new ideas and try to adopt a test-and-learn approach. It is good to be experimental in business, given that you make use of your experience, business acumen, intuition, vision, strategies and preparedness. This experiment should not be baseless and should be made taking calculated risks into account. Sometimes you can take a big leap in business when you are experimental in nature.

Process-based Approach: Your business activities must be divided into functions and their processes. When you follow a process-based approach, your team has transparency about the attainment of the goals by being made aware of the series of steps or processes. When these processes are written, controlled and implemented, you will save lot of time. Make your business faster with a process-based approach.

Sales Reward and Recognition: Create a culture of employee recognition programmes within your business. Appreciate the top performers with gifts, promotions and incentives when they achieve sales targets and exhibit good performance. Building a culture of appreciation is part of a positive work culture and attracts good talent too. Your sales reward and recognition policies can make your business faster by encouraging more productivity, innovative ideas, more efficiency and more loyalty, adding to your business wealth.

Strategic Partnership and Acquisition: As a businessman, you have a lot of goals on your plate. The best way to grow is to develop partnerships. Identify your strategic partners and collaborate to meet larger business goals. Look for synergy and tie up with other commercial players. You can reduce competition through the acquisition of other locally operating businesses. Similarly, you can develop a new product or service, reach new markets by building mutually beneficial relationships and by understanding your strategic partner well. Partnerships are a great way to strengthen the position of small and big businesses.

Reachability and Accessibility: Think big and create solutions for the country and world at large. Your revenue will grow multifold and your customer base will increase exponentially. Develop a communications channel for all the stakeholders of your products and services. Make sure they feel comfortable, right from pre-sales to post-sales. Ensure your presence on different social media platforms to increase customer interaction and engagement. These simple steps will help you grow the business quickly.

PHYSICAL AGE MAKES YOU SLOW, AGE OF YOUR BUSINESS MAKES YOU FAST

Good Financial Health: Your organization's financial health is an indicator of your business performance. When you seek investors, check your business health financially. Liquidity, profitability, solvency and operational efficiency are the four pillars that determine your financial health and must be considered in tandem. If your business is healthy and attractive, you can make your business fast. Remember that your capital structure should be balanced to avoid situations like financial distress; if it has components of debt, it is not healthy. Additionally, try to find various channels that will enable you to infuse capital into your business portfolio, making sure liquidity is maintained.

Franchise Approach: It is good to work on franchise model in business, as long as it is feasible in your business activity. Franchising has many advantages. You can spread your brand story at a fast pace through a network of brand ambassadors who share your vision. You are able to scale up operations and attain economies of scale in less time. While franchising, you can learn from the franchisee knowledge base while dealing with day-to-day challenges and providing customized support. To do this, however, you must consider a franchising model; please take your time to understand probable impact of the COCO (company-owned company-operated) model, FOCO (franchise-owned company-operated) model and FOFO (franchise-owned franchise-operated) model of franchising.

You must consider the nature of your business, your resources and your talent pool while making your business fast and consistent.

35

SHABRI, THE DOCTOR AND THE CCTV

Shabri was a tribal woman who loved nature. At her wedding, many animals had to be killed as part of a ritual. Shabri opposed this practice and wanted to save the animals. She requested her mother to stop this age-old tradition, but she failed in doing so. So she left her home and started living in the forest.

Shabri was a seeker of knowledge and wanted to pursue the path of spirituality. She frequently searched for a guru or a teacher, but was not accepted as a disciple by anyone due to her tribal background. One day, she reached the ashram of Sage Matanga who was impressed by her dedication and behaviour and thus took her in as a student. Shabri happily lived there, learning and working for many years. Both Shabri and Sage Matanga grew old in time. Before leaving his body, Matanga blessed Shabri for her hard work and told her to wait for Lord Rama when she expressed her wish to meet the lord. And thereafter, Shabri started to wait for the Lord to arrive. Every day, Shabri kept the ashram tidy, plucked fresh fruits and was ready to host.

Finally, Shabri's wait was over. Lord Rama arrived in the ashram with his brother Lakshmana while travelling from one place to another in search of his wife, Sita. Shabri was speechless and overwhelmed by Rama's presence and bowed with love. Then, she rushed to pluck the best fruits from the forest. Before offering them to Lord Rama, she took small bites of every fruit to check their sweetness. Out of compassion, she served the Lord only the fruits that tasted the sweetest. Rama munched on the juicy feast.

On the other hand, Lakshmana considered shabri's behaviour as insult and did not understand the mindset of the old woman. Lord Rama, however, saw it as an expression of true love and devotion and told Lakshmana that Shabri wanted to keep aside all the bitter fruits.

This meeting between Shabri and Lord Rama is one of the most heartwarming tales in the Ramayana.

Entrepreneurs are not blessed with a devotee like Shabri, one who will check the options and shortlist the best for them. But our businesses too need a righteous force like Shabri to recommend the best! It is possible that few options bring a bitter experience and lessons for the future, while only few others lead to sweet experiences and high performance. A businessman must have a Shabri-like option to check viability of projects, products and services. Make your *people, processes and business practices your Shabri,* which can then analyse and evaluate the potential outcomes of any project or venture. The reviews given by customers on social media about your business or products and services are like your own Shabri. You can work according to these reviews and plan strategies.

It is said that the wellness of an individual is attained by eating right, a healthy lifestyle, right thoughts and by being in the right environment. We still visit a doctor for regular health check-ups and to diagnose our problems. Here, the doctor is like a subject expert who guides and suggests advice on the basis of health conditions. He evaluates the condition critically based on his specialized knowledge and experiences. Your business also needs doctors to watch its present and future health based on numbers. They check indicators, like earnings before interest, taxes, depreciation, and amortization (EBITDA), to diagnose the real situation. These doctors are instrumental in recommending corrective action and preventive action (also known as CAPA in any area of business).

Identify the doctors in your business.

In general, they are accounting professionals, legal experts, departmental heads, subject matter experts and consultants who have extensive knowledge in their domain and can individually check the business health in terms of their expertise in quality, debt management, cost management, ethics, compliance, pricing, taxes, profits, project deliverables, timelines and a lot more. These doctors help you restore the health of your business. They prescribe the right medication and keep you informed about the advantages, disadvantages, risks and alternatives regarding a proposed treatment. Allow them to do their duty. Let them take the appropriate steps to make the right diagnosis using different tools, to provide treatment and to follow up on the progress.

Similarly, a CCTV is the symbol of your extended visibility. With simple checks and precautionary measures, you can keep a check on your own actions. At the same time, you need to check unwanted threats to the business that may be caused by the actions and intent of others. To guard your business, increase the reachability of your vision/sight. Your CCTV works like a mirror that gives you a complete picture of reality. You may then accordingly understand what to do and what not to do. When deep-diving into these issues, you will learn for the future and be able to identify the areas where changes have to be implemented. Your CCTV is your guiding force; it monitors operations and keeps your business safe.

Don't you think that minimum (yet significant) preparedness with Shabri, the doctor and the CCTV can keep a check on the wellness of your organization? Identify your Shabri to seek guidance. Identify the doctors to make your business healthy. Identify security needs and other measures to increase the scale of your business and make it grow.

3Fs OF BUSINESS—FRIENDS, FAITH AND FUTURE

36

I DIDN'T MEAN TO SAY THAT

How often do you hear, 'No. I didn't mean to say that'?

It is quite common to hear people say that they did not actually mean to say what was inferred or understood by the other person. On many occasions, it is thought that the other has misconstrued and twisted the words to mean something that was not intended. On other occasions, it is misunderstood. We refer to these situations as a communication gap. Why are these instances so very common in our lives?

Before I provide an answer, let me narrate a small incident.

Once upon a time, a traveller came across three bricklayers who were engaged in laying bricks on a vast plot of land by the road. The traveller walked up to the first man and asked him, 'What are you doing?'

The bricklayer replied, 'Can't you see that I am laying bricks?'

The traveller approached the second man and asked him the same question.

The second man replied, 'I am laying bricks in order to earn a living for my family.'

The traveller then walked up to the third bricklayer and asked him the same question again. The third man smiled upon the traveller.

'I am building a world-class school for children from the neighbouring villages to study here. They will be the shapers of their world in the future,' he said.

All three of these men were laying the same bricks, but their replies were divergent. It is evident that all the three men came from similar social backgrounds, were all working at the site to earn a living and yet their replies differed. Each of the three replies conveyed altogether different things to the traveller. What can we learn from this story?

When we talk about communication, its meaning and relevance is not simply confined to writing, speaking or listening. Communication transcends these and is the lifeblood of your business.

Consider the names of brands. When a businessman selling tea names his shop 'Chaayos' or 'Chai Point', for instance, then it is perfect brand communication. Similarly, when a samosa and snacks' seller, opts for a name like Samiyosa, or when coffee shops name their outlets as Café Coffee Day and when a pre-primary school's name is Bachpan, Brand communication has done it job.

Remember that your brand name and the many ways you choose to popularize this name are extremely important. Brand architecture of your product/services is always important and must be an integral part of your business strategy. Choose a perfect brand name for your products and services. Think of an attractive punchline that explains your brand or its services easily or highlights its qualities. The colour theory must be selected keeping in view the age and interests of your customers and the market trends. Remember that signages are your medium of communication with the outside world. If your inner communication is strong, it creates a long-lasting impact. Further, the choice of fonts, style, packaging must be eye-catching for your customers.

Other factors too play a vital role. For instance, your presence on social media handles can be used as a tool for promotion, or to keep customers informed on the latest updates on products, services, support or even to engage with them. Your business ought to have a storyline and a brand ambassador to promote your business.

Think about it. Small changes lead to a bigger impact.

Your advertisement and its storyline can convey many things to the right audience.

Remember to be firm and deliberate in crafting this brand image so the miscommunication can be avoided. Link your brand to its marketing and watch it soar.

There is another integral part of brand communication. This has taken shape in recent years and it is highly effective. For instance, content-rich immersive videos, witty tweets, infographics, article posts are instrumental in customer engagement. Earlier the trend and demand were limited to product-related communication. Today, customer-oriented communication strategies are the game changer. Content marketing through various digital communication platforms is key for brand-building. Effective communication can open new routes of revenue generation without any geographical limitation. If you plan well, your product can reach millions of people globally.

The benefit of strong communication has examples in Bollywood as well. The title 'angry young man' suited Amitabh Bachchan perfectly at one point in time. Similarly, the title of 'larger than life' goes well with

COMMUNICATION —THE LORD OF SUCCESS

Salman Khan now. This is so because of the communication established by these film stars with their respective audiences through films in the last few decades. As a result of this, film producers or directors ended up casting them in stories that matched the description.

GRATITUDE

This book will not be complete without expressing my gratitude to the people who stood by me.

I am grateful to my mother Savitri Gupta who instilled not only good values, but also life skills in me. These lessons helped me build a stronger relationship with everyone in our big joint family. I thank my father S.K. Gupta for believing in my abilities at all times. Thank you Mummy and Papa for nurturing me like a normal child and filling my life with love and making me understand the importance of spreading love.

My wife Deepshikha has been the rock in my life for the last 34 years. She nurtured our family while I pursued my passion of building an enterprise. My dreams have been fuelled by her.

My daughter Dr Aakanksha not only kept diagnosing the book's health, but also gave timely prescriptions for its betterment. My lawyer son Aakash evaluated the book on merits and argued on what needs to be there in the book. My children have helped me grow wings to fly.

I deeply thank Tijay for being the Lakshmana of my life. He stood with me and always supported me in all professional and personal decisions. I thank Vijay, Anjali Garg, Satish Garg, Pooja and Ria who kept faith in my ideas, my principles and initiatives.

I thank my mentor the late Dr Mahesh Gupta for lessons in life, business and humanity. I am grateful to Rakesh Aggarwal who has always inspired me with his wisdom and values. He is one of the most hard-working people I know. I thank my young friend Sahil Aggarwal for being my ready reckoner on just about everything. He always has far-sighted beliefs and stimulating thoughts.

I thank my friends Ajay Purohit, Pawan Sabharwal and K.S. Kohli for always encouraging me.

I thank the disruptive minds of my think tank—N.K. Jain, Krishan Sharma, Rosy Ahuja, Deepak Deopa, Uma Devi Subraveti and Anamika Chadha. Their diverse thoughts, innovative ideas, workable solutions and aggressive strategies have combined seamlessly with my vision. With time, we have learnt to hold hands tightly through thick and thin.

I thank my extended family of 1200 playschools and 110 formal school partners. I also express gratitude towards K. Roopa Reddy and K. Sreekanth Reddy for their unconditional support.

I am grateful to Devendra Mathur for his initial handholding during the writing of this book. I thank Girish Makwana and Nisha Sharma for living this dream with me, for their valuable and thoughtful inputs in creating this book.

My special thanks to Dibakar Ghosh and the entire team of Rupa Publications for guiding me throughout the publication process.

My business associates H.P. Mangla, Anil Garg, Amit Satpal Gupta, Daksh Gupta, Rahul Mangla, Amit Gupta, Chartered Accountant (CA) Anil Gupta, Naveen Breja and Bhavesh Aggarwal have always reposed their faith in me and worked hard to achieve the goals we have set for ourselves.

I value everyone's contribution in my life and I am committed to take the learning forward in all future endeavours.

www.ingramcontent.com/pod-product-compliance
Lightning Source LLC
LaVergne TN
LVHW090512110826
845146LV00003B/833

* 9 7 8 9 3 9 1 2 5 6 6 5 4 *